Beyond submission

Rudolf Kutschera

Beyond submission

A theological response to Islam

PETER LANG

**Bibliographic Information published by the
Deutsche Nationalbibliothek**
The Deutsche Nationalbibliothek lists this publication in the Deutsche
Nationalbibliografie; detailed bibliographic data is available online at
http://dnb.d-nb.de.

Library of Congress Cataloging-in-Publication Data
A CIP catalog record for this book has been applied for at the
Library of Congress.

ISBN 978-3-631-88389-1
E-ISBN 978-3-631-88391-4 (E-PDF)
E-ISBN 978-3-631-88392-1 (EPUB)
DOI 10.3726/b19928

© Peter Lang GmbH
Internationaler Verlag der Wissenschaften
Berlin 2022
All rights reserved.

Peter Lang – Berlin · Bern · Bruxelles · New York · Oxford · Warszawa · Wien

All parts of this publication are protected by copyright. Any
utilisation outside the strict limits of the copyright law, without
the permission of the publisher, is forbidden and liable to
prosecution. This applies in particular to reproductions,
translations, microfilming, and storage and processing in
electronic retrieval systems.

This publication has been peer reviewed.

www.peterlang.com

Abstract

This book examines central theological aspects of the Qur'an and of Islam. Its four chapters seek to present certain key insights of contemporary Islamic Studies in a way that is accessible to a non-specialist public.

The first chapter examines the sources of the Qur'an, which can be identified both in the "forma mentis" (mindset) reflected in the Qur'an and in textual parallels derived from Judeo-Christian, Manichaean, Byzantine, Nestorian and Roman elements. This perspective casts a new light on the specifically Islamic accent of the Qur'an.

The question of Anti-Judaism in the Qur'an, considered in the second chapter, compares the way in which central biblical figures such as Abraham and Moses are depicted in the Tanakh/Old Testament and in the Qur'an. This leads to the conclusion that it is essential for meaningful Christian-Muslim dialogue that Jewish voices always be included.

A critical examination of the Qur'anic presentation of Jesus in the third chapter reveals its interest in transforming Jesus and other biblical figures into precursors of Muhammad. The theological answer for an appropriate understanding of Jesus in the face of Islam lies in rediscovering both the Jewish tradition and forgotten aspects of Church dogma, which were clarified at the same time as the Qur'an was written.

The fourth chapter presents two little-known views on Islam: that of the German Jewish philosopher Franz Rosenzweig (1886–1929) and that of Pope emeritus Benedict XVI (*1927), as set out in his lecture at the University of Regensburg/Germany in 2006. With great candor and integrity, both authors try to get to the heart of the theological questions raised by Islam, thereby contributing decisively to a rationally justifiable response.

Table of Contents

Foreword 11

1. The sources of the Qur'an 15

  1.1 The Qur'an in its historical context 15
      Muhammad and the Qur'an 15
      The literary character of the Qur'an 17
      Christian and Jewish influences 18
      A realistic view of the origin of the Qur'an 20
      The question of the sources of the Qur'an 22

  1.2 Jewish Christian traces 23
      Indications of Jewish Christian influences 23
      The Seal of the Prophets
      and the sending of an angel 25
      The accusation of the falsification
      of the scriptures 27
      Identifiable sources 28
      The relevance of the question
      of Jewish Christian influences 29

  1.3 Manichaean elements 30
      Manichaeism in the context
      of the emerging Islam 30
      Manichaean textual references in the Qur'an 31
      Convergence and divergence in content 32

  1.4 Further influences on the Qur'an
     and emerging Islam 33

    The unity of politics and religion
    in the Byzantine Empire 33
    Theological divisions within Christianity 34
    Theological analogies
    between Islam and Nestorianism 36
    Influences of ancient Roman legal thought 38

1.5 The specific Islamic accent 42
    Traditional judgments of Christian theologians
    on the Qur'an 42
    The combination of poetry
    and a sense of superiority 43
    The specifically Islamic theological emphasis 44

2. Anti-Judaism in the Qur'an? 48

2.1 The seriousness of the question 48
    Two current examples 48
    An illustrative Qur'anic verse 49
    The transformation of biblical content
    in the Qur'an 50
    Statements in the Qur'an on the plurality
    of religions 52

2.2 Abraham and Moses in the Qur'an 54
    From the biblical Abraham
    to the prototype of the pious Muslim 54
    Moses–from biblical lawgiver
    to Qur'anic accuser of the Jews 58

2.3 Phases in the relationships with the Jews 60

2.4 Questions concerning Qur'anic Anti-Judaism 65

Table of Contents

Inner-Islamic approaches	65
An example of a Jewish voice on the Qur'an	66
A commission from a Christian perspective	67

3. Jesus in the Qur'an ... 70

3.1 Sources of the Qur'anic image of Jesus ... 70
The recourse to apocryphal sources ... 70
Theological voluntarism
in the apocryphal sources ... 72

3.2 Basic features of the Qur'anic perception of Jesus ... 75
Representations of Jesus ... 75
The defense speech of the infant Jesus in Sura 19 ... 76
Jesus as a prefiguration of Muhammad and a prophetic model ... 77
The rejection of the crucifixion of Jesus ... 78
The recourse to Docetism ... 79
Jesus as the eschatological accuser of the Christians ... 81

3.3 Qur'anic argumentation against the divinity of Jesus ... 82
Argumentation patterns ... 82
The title "Son of God" ... 83

3.4 Jesus in current Muslim-Christian thinking ... 85
The approach of Comparative Theology ... 85
The Comparative Approach
and the Qur'anic question about Jesus ... 86

Questions on the Comparative Approach 89

3.5 A Deeper Understanding of Jesus 91
The challenge of cultural diversity 91
The tradition of Israel as corrective 92
The rediscovered unification
of divine and human free will in Jesus 95

4. Franz Rosenzweig and Joseph Ratzinger on Islam 99

4.1 Islam as an overall phenomenon 99

4.2 Franz Rosenzweig's view on Islam 101
Biographical context 101
Natural paganism in the form of revelation 102
The absence of "inner conversion" 104
The oriental despot 105
Parallels to an Inner-Islamic reform movement .. 107
Redemption and revelation 108
A different realm of religious knowledge 111
Conclusions from Rosenzweig's insights 112

4.3 The Regensburg lecture of Pope Benedict XVI ... 114
Context of the speech 114
The vastness of reason 116
Deepening our knowledge of God 118
Obstacles to understanding 119

4.4 Summary and outlook 122

Bibliography 124

Foreword

The word *Islam* can be translated as '*submission*'–although other translations may also be possible–and the bedrock of this submission is the Qur'an. Is it possible to look at Islam without also succumbing to its internal logic of submission? *Beyond Submission* attempts to do just that, and is the fruit of several years of theological study of Islam. The author is a theologian committed to the values of personal liberty and human dignity generated by the biblical and Western tradition.

The public discussion about Islam oscillates between trivializing the subject and demonizing its adherents. How can one engage with the topic while avoiding these extremes?

This book examines some of the key issues and perspectives in contemporary Islamic studies and seeks to make them accessible to a non-specialist audience. In doing so, it also confronts issues which, by the logic of submission and "politically correct" conventions, are not mentioned at all.

Engaging with Islam at the *theological* level thus requires that issues of day-to-day politics be set aside. However, this approach is also largely frowned upon, suspected of signaling a return to the unfortunate religious comparisons and associated polemics of the past.

But it was Muhammad himself who launched a theological program, which is why the Qur'an addresses Christians and Jews directly in innumerable passages. So why should one not attempt to engage with the Qur'an and Islam at the *theological* level?

With this end in view, four themes have been chosen for discussion:

– The sources of the Qur'an and other factors which have influenced its genesis.

- How the pervasive Anti-Judaism in the Qur'an has shaped relationships with the Jews to this day.
- How Jesus is perceived in the Qur'an and the questions this raises for Christians.
- Two philosophical-theological attempts to respond to the major issues raised by Islam as a whole.

This book is therefore not an introduction to Islam and is not conceived as a special contribution to Islamic studies. It is not a discussion of socio-political questions about Islam, nor a comparison of religions.

The following example serves to illustrate the book's selection of topics and its perspective *beyond submission*: Muhammad followed the growth of his community and his family with keen interest. His adoptive son, Zayd, married a beautiful woman and brought her home. Was she to be denied to Muhammad, the appointed Prophet of Allāh? In the fourth year of the Islamic era, Muhammad saw Zayd's wife "unveiled and immediately succumbed to her charms. He urged his adopted son to separate from her and then married her."[1] That is why, in Sura 33 of the Qur'an, a "divine" word is conveyed to Muhammad and to all those after him who find themselves in a similar situation: "It is not for a believing man or a believing woman, when Allāh and His Messenger have decided a matter, that they should [thereafter] have any choice about their affair... So when Zayd had no longer any need for her, We [= Allāh] married her to

---

1 Nagel, Tilman: Was ist der Islam? Grundzüge einer Weltreligion [What is Islam? Basic Features of a World Religion]. Duncker&Humblot: Berlin 2018, p. 127. All translations from Non-English sources are by the author or his collaborators.

you [= the Prophet Mohammad] ... And ever is the command of Allāh accomplished."[2]

This excerpt from the Qur'an shows that "Allāh's Decree" apparently legitimizes a right of access to all persons, a "right" which was accordingly practiced in respect of the adherents of all the religions and traditions that predated Islam.

There is an urgent need to clarify these issues from a historical and a theological point of view. Their continuing relevance is highlighted by an observation of the German-Jewish philosopher Franz Rosenzweig that the confrontation with Islam would shape the third millennium.

---

[2] Sura 33:36–37 (excerpts); most translations, like the one quoted above, suggest that Zayd would have wanted a divorce of his own initiative. The context, however, leaves open whether this is an interpretative addition serving to absolve Muhammad from potentially dubious moral behavior.

1. The sources of the Qur'an

1.1 The Qur'an in its historical context

Muhammad and the Qur'an

Islam originated on the Arabian Peninsula in the 7th century AD, thus, from a European perspective, in the period of late antiquity. The trade routes to Jewish and Christian settlements were a central part of the world of the widely travelled trader "Muhammad"[3] (570–632), designated a Prophet in the Islamic context. Even if many biographical details concerning Muhammad remain controversial to this day,[4] they are of little relevance for a *theological* discussion of the Qur'an and Islam today. However, the following key data about Muhammad's life provide a useful background:

570 AD: Born in Mecca, orphaned at an early age, travels extensively for purposes of trade
595: Marriage to the wealthy widowed businesswoman, Khadija
610: First mystical visions
619: Death of Khadija and clan-related conflicts in Mecca

---

[3] In keeping with numerous Islamic works, the linguistic form "Muhammad" is used here. Except for quotations, other Arabic names and terms are mostly reproduced in their usual German or English forms.

[4] The first biography of Muhammad was written about one hundred years after his death and shows clear signs of painting an idealized picture. Nevertheless, one can assume–with the majority of contemporary Western Qur'anic scholars–that these basic biographical data are fundamentally correct. Studies that are completely at odds with this can therefore be regarded as irrelevant.

622: Emigration (Hegira/Hijra) to Medina–beginning of the Muslim era

624–627: Growth of the community, raids against caravans and battles against Mecca

628: Subjugation of the Jews of Khaybar after a devastating siege and battle

630: Muhammad and his army enter Mecca

632: Death of Muhammad

The Qur'an reflects the dramatic struggle of Muhammad and his first Muslim community to gain acceptance of the new doctrine. Accordingly, Qur'anic editions[5] usually distinguish the "Meccan" suras from the "Medinan" suras.[6]

While up to the 20th century interest centered on the person of Muhammad as author of the Qur'an, more recent Qur'anic research attributes at least as important a role to the emerging Muslim *community* in the creation of the Qur'an.[7] The biographical stages of Muhammad's life and the developmental phases of his community are clearly reflected in the Qur'anic depiction of biblical figures.[8] After Muhammad's death, further

---

[5] Unless otherwise specified, the English translation of the Qur'an quoted here is the Ṣaḥeeḥ International Translation, available online at https://asimiqbal2nd.files.wordpress.com/2009/06/quran-sahih-international.pdf.

[6] Often a more precise differentiation is made between early, middle and late Meccan suras. However, this has little relevance for an understanding of the contents of the Qur'an, since the majority of those who read and listen to the Qur'an accept its contents irrespective of their dating or classification.

[7] Cf. especially: Neuwirth, Angelika: The Qur'an and Late Antiquity: A Shared Heritage. Oxford University Press: New York 2019. This is considered a standard work for the historical-literary approach to the Qur'an.

[8] Cf. chapters 2 and 3 of this book.

revisions of the Qur'anic text followed until the final edit about a century later.[9]

The literary character of the Qur'an

The Arabic word "Qur'an" can be translated as "reading" and points to the liturgical context of its origins. It contains many references to the biblical Psalms. From a literary point of view, the Qur'an can be characterized as "appellatory persuasive speech."[10] This can be seen in the almost continuous use of the second-person "you" form of address, emanating from a transcendent "I" or "we"–signifying Allāh–and addressed to a "proclaimer", "who in turn addresses a hearership."[11] It is thus a kind of drama on two levels: "Allāh" speaks as a protagonist in the drama–and is at the same time a figure whose words and actions are reported. This ever-changing scenario may at first confuse the reader who may be inclined to compare the text of the Qur'an with that of the Bible. Within this apparent confusion of voices, it is possible, however, to identify quite specific sources of the Qur'an and influences on it. They will be examined in further detail below.

---

9 Various controversial questions about the genesis, literary idiosyncrasy or authorship of the (Sunni) Qur'an can be ignored here. Relevant as source of Sunni-Muslim faith–that is, for about 90 percent of all Muslims–is the final text with its 114 suras (= chapters). For the sake of simplicity, Muhammad is mostly cited in this work as the author of the Qur'an, although a number of other authors and editors from the circle of the emerging Muslim community were involved until the final text was produced.

10 Neuwirth 2019, p. 348.

11 Neuwirth 2019, p. 348. Here we also find further detailed references to this "multilayered scenario of communication and interaction" in the Qur'an.

Christian and Jewish influences

The religious landscape of Arabia at the time of Muhammad was very diverse. Despite the dominant polytheism, there were also Christians–both isolated individuals and those gathered in settlements–as well as larger Jewish settlements in and around Medina.

Under Greek influence, a small section of the population in Syria and Palestine, that is, in the northern part of the Arabian Peninsula, belonged to the Byzantine imperial church. The native inhabitants there, however, were mostly "Monophysites." This means that, like many oriental Christians to this day, they recognized only the *divine* nature of Jesus. Muhammad, therefore, did not become acquainted with Christianity in its "Chalcedonian" form, that is to say, in the form officially recognized by the Church,[12] but rather in various heretical forms.[13]

No systematic Christian missionary work had yet been undertaken on the Arab peninsula, but there were monks or hermits who had settled in the desert. They were primarily those "who had a falling out with their church for dogmatic or disciplinary reasons and had sought refuge in the desert."[14] Probably there were also Christian merchants along the trade routes. Contemporary accounts mention Christians like, for

---

12 It was decreed at the Council of Chalcedon in 451 that both the divine and the human natures were present "unconfusedly, unchangeably, indivisibly, and inseparably" in Jesus. This article of faith is still decisive for the major Christian churches today.

13 Cf. Simon, Róbert: Mani and Muhammad. JSAI (Jerusalem Studies in Arabic and Islam) 21: Jerusalem 1997, p. 127.

14 Busse, Heribert: Islam, Judaism and Christianity: Theological and Historical Affiliations. Markus Wiener Publishers: Princeton, N.J. 1998, p. 13.

example, a Coptic carpenter who built the roof of the Kaaba around 605. It can also be assumed that itinerant Christian preachers, perhaps from southern Arabia, frequented the markets during the various pilgrimage festivals and that encounters with such people provided a major impetus for Muhammad's preaching.[15]

Muhammad and his fellow believers obtained information about Christianity mostly from oral traditions, most likely from their participation in religious services and religious disputes. Therefore, the identification of "reference texts" or "sources" of the Qur'an faces a fundamental problem: oral traditions were on the whole not transformed into written documents. Consequently, the reconstruction of these sources depends on the few preserved written texts. Biblical and post-biblical texts and narratives found their way into the Qur'an almost entirely through the filter of oral transmission. The authors of the Qur'an relied on the biblical knowledge of their audience or readers– even if only on the basis of hearsay–and they then proceeded to impose their own interpretation on the biblical material.[16]

The Qur'an reflects in detail the disputes with Jews that took place especially in Medina. For that reason, biblical texts found their way into the Qur'an "very often through the exegesis of rabbinical traditions"[17] or in the form of Jewish and Christian

---

15 Cf. Andrae, Tor: Der Ursprung des Islams und das Christentum [The Origin of Islam and Christianity]. Almquist&Wiksells: Uppsala, 1926 [Hildesheim: ²1977], p. 201.
16 Cf. Reynolds, Gabriel Said: The Qur'an and Its Biblical Subtext. Routledge: London, 2010, p. 2.
17 Neuwirth, Angelika: Im vollen Licht der Geschichte [In the Full Light of History]. In Hartwig, Dirk et al.: "Im vollen Licht der Geschichte." Ergon: Würzburg 2008, p. 29.

apocrypha.[18] Biblical influences on the Qur'an are thus in essence *mediated* influences. The Bible in the Qur'an is consistently an "interpreted Bible,"[19] in that it mostly reflects Jewish or Christian interpretations which have been given a specifically Islamic orientation.

A realistic view of the origin of the Qur'an

The wealth of literary and biblical reference texts within the Qur'an shows that its origin is by no means due to the mystical inspiration experienced by a seer in the solitude of the desert who may have had occasional contact with Jews or Christians. "We do not assume an 'author' behind the Qur'an, but rather– apart from the [chronologically] very first suras, which reflect an individual conversation between God and man–a protracted communal discussion that lasts over the whole period of the Prophet's ministry."[20] Both the source texts and the discussions were then summarized and edited by a charismatic figure and consolidated into a final, definitive text after the death of Muhammad, most probably still in the 7th century.[21]

---

18 This refers to post-Biblical or extra-Biblical writings of the Jewish or Christian tradition. Cf. also section 3.1 Sources of the Qur'anic image of Jesus.

19 The renowned Islamic researcher, Sidney H. Griffith (b. 1938), uses the expression "interpreted Bible" to summarize his research on the Bible in the Qur'an, for example in: Reynolds, Gabriel Said (Ed.): The Qur'ān in Its Historical Context. Routledge: London 2008, pp. 109–137.

20 Neuwirth 2019, p. 17.

21 Neuwirth, after reviewing various theories of the origin of the Qur'an, comes to the following conclusion: "The assumption that the Qur'an, transmitted above all orally in the various centers of the emerging [Islamic] realm, obtained a binding textual form ... perhaps around 655 [i.e. during the reign of the third caliph

The Qur'an itself categorically rejects the supposition that Muhammad obtained information from certain sources,[22] emphasizing that Muhammad could neither read nor write,[23] and thus establishing Allāh himself, i.e. the divine inspiration conveyed by the archangel Gabriel, taken from the biblical tradition,[24] as the source of Muhammad's preaching. From the Muslim side, this has given rise to a fundamental skepticism, which persists to this day, with regard to the literary-critical and historical research into the Qur'anic text. Moreover, the Muslim interpretation of the Qur'an always emphasizes the *general* meaning of a Qur'anic verse over a *specific* interpretation shaped by the context in which it was written.[25]

As these Muslim positions make an open discussion on the origins of the Qur'an difficult, it is all the more necessary to

---

'Uthmān] but at the latest in the reign of 'Abd al-Malik [an important Umayyad caliph] around 690, can no longer be dismissed out of hand." (Neuwirth 2019, p. 149).

22 Cf. Sura 16:103 where, apart from this rejection of non-Qur'anic sources, it is also determined that only Arabic can be considered a divine source of revelation: "And We certainly know that they say, 'It is only a human being who teaches him [i.e. the Prophet].' The tongue of the one they refer to is foreign, and this recitation, i.e. Qur'an] is [in] a clear Arabic language."

23 Cf. Sura 29:48: "And you [= the Prophet Muhammad] did not recite before it any scripture, nor did you inscribe one with your right hand. Otherwise the falsifiers would have had [cause for] doubt."

24 Cf. Sura 2:97, one of the three Sura verses in which Gabriel (in Arabic: Jibril) is mentioned in the Qur'an: "Gabriel–it is [none but] he who has brought it [i.e. the Qur'an] down upon your heart, [O Muhammad], by permission of Allāh."

25 This is how the Islamic philosopher of religion, Shabbir Akhtar, summarizes the basic orientation of Islamic Qur'anic exegesis. (in: Akhtar, Shabbir: Islam as Political Religion. Routledge: London 2011, p. 169).

move *beyond submission* in order to arrive at a realistic view of the sources of the Qur'an. The biblical sources occupy a prominent position here.

The question of the sources of the Qur'an

The German-Jewish Islamic scholar, Heinrich Speyer (1897–1935), lists in his fundamental work on *The biblical narratives of the Qur'an* a total of 164 Biblical textual references within the Qur'an. He groups them into Jewish and Christian apocrypha on the one hand, and into Jewish and Christian literature on the other.[26] In doing so, he diagnoses a "surprising interweaving of biblical and post-biblical stories" and notes that many Qur'anic verses "attempt to imitate the Psalms or, more likely still, Christian homilies."[27]

Speyer's work follows the tradition of Qur'anic research initiated by Abraham Geiger with his dissertation *What did Muhammad absorb from Judaism?* (1833). While Geiger, like other authors in the centuries before him, had proceeded on the assumption that Muhammad was the author of the Qur'an, it had in the meanwhile become generally accepted "that the Qur'an is the result of a dynamic, complex communication process."[28] This complexity consequently also excludes the possibility that the Qur'an could be regarded one-dimensionally as a copy of Jewish or Christian models. Related hypotheses–such as positing a Syrian-Aramaic text as a precursor to the Qur'an–must be relegated to the realm of speculation.[29] They

---

26 Cf. Speyer: Heinrich: Die biblischen Erzählungen im Qoran [The biblical narratives of the Qur'an]. Olms: Hildesheim 2013, pp. 502–505.
27 Speyer 2013, p. 463 f.
28 Neuwirth 2019, p. 48.
29 More on this in Neuwirth 2019, p. 54.

are also problematic because they would ultimately render superfluous a critical analysis of the *content* of the Qur'an.

All in all, it is clear from current Qur'anic research that a multitude of influences, including those from Arabic literature, have had an impact on the Qur'anic text. These can now be identified relatively precisely, and in some detail.[30]

In summary it can be said that the scenario so eagerly described by Islamic sources of a barren desert landscape, primarily populated by culturally alien Bedouins, which "Islamic tradition equates with Jāhiliyā, with 'barbarism,' the dark backdrop to Islam which stands in the bright light of history,"[31] in fact never existed at all.

In what follows we shall examine more closely those influences on the Qur'an that are most relevant for the theological interpretation of its message.

1.2 Jewish Christian traces

Indications of Jewish Christian influences

Among the sources of the Qur'an and Islam, Jewish Christian influences stand out in a special way.[32] This is already apparent

---

30 The research project of the Berlin-Brandenburg Academy of Sciences and Humanities deserves special mention here. It provides a comprehensive online commentary on the Qur'an (available at: corpuscoranicum.de). Many Qur'anic verses are linked with texts from the historical environment, making it possible to determine their original context.

31 Marx, Michael: Zur Programmatik des Akademienvorhabens Corpus Coranicum [On the Program of the Academy Project Corpus Coranicum]. In: Hartwig 2008, p. 41 ff.

32 Cf. Colpe, Carsten: Das Siegel der Propheten: Historische Beziehungen zwischen antikem Judentum, Judenchristentum,

from the origin of the word "Nasir," Arabic for "Christian." Presumably, it referred originally to Jewish Christian groups known as "Nazoreans." The term "Jewish Christian" was generally applied to those Jewish groups and theological currents that accepted Jesus as the Messiah of Israel, while remaining fully Jewish. These groups, which within early Christianity soon drifted into or were nudged into heresy, reflect the dramatic and centuries-long struggle for an adequate definition of the relationship between Judaism and Christianity.

Research into these influences on the Qur'an has a long history[33] and supports the following conclusions: the origins of the Qur'an should not be attributed to only *one* specific Jewish Christian source, but rather to a slow "process of assimilation of disparate elements"[34] of what could broadly be termed Jewish

---

Heidentum und frühem Islam [The Seal of the Prophets: Historical relations between ancient Judaism, Jewish Christianity, Paganism and early Islam]. Arbeiten zur neutestamentlichen Theologie und Zeitgeschichte. ANTZ Volume 3: Berlin 2006. Here (cf. p. 29 ff.) Colpe problematizes the expression "Jewish Christian" as a term originating in German scientific language, which only incompletely reflects the complex development of this "movement." Nevertheless, it is helpful as a collective term as long as one keeps in mind the diversity of "Jewish Christianity" as a whole.

33 So, for example, the Protestant theologian Adolf von Harnack (1851–1930) defined Islam as a whole as a form of Gnostic Jewish Christianity. In: Harnack, Adolf von: Lehrbuch der Dogmengeschichte [The History of Dogma]. Mohr: Tübingen 1909, II, p. 537.

34 Roncaglia, M.P.: Élements Ébionites et Elkésaites dans le Coran [Ebionite and Elchasaite Elements in the Qur'an]. In: POC (Proche Orient Chrétien) 21: Jersusalem 1971, pp. 101–126. The author refers primarily to textual evidence from Epiphanius' *Panarion*, to the pseudo-Clementines clearly identifiable as Jewish Christian, and to Eusebius' Ecclesiastical History.

Christianity, which actually encompassed a variety of forms. In particular, Arab Judaism may still have been permeated by a Jewish Christian variant even up to the time of the emergence of Islam in the 7th century.[35] This is a most astonishing fact, because research has generally regarded the final separation of Judaism and Christianity as having been completed with the 4th century.

External indications of the existence of such influences are to be found in certain ritual elements such as the frequent ablutions before prayers in Islam. It is noticeable that "these practices were also common among the Ebionites and the Elchasaites [= two Jewish Christian sects]."[36] Remarkably, Muhammad was therefore also suspected by his pagan opponents of being "Sabaean/Sabian".[37]

The Seal of the Prophets and the sending of an angel

In analogy to Jewish Christian sources, the Qur'an repeatedly mentions certain series of prophets with biblical names. Accordingly, the designation of Muhammad as "Seal of the Prophets"–mentioned in the Qur'an in Sura 33:40[38]–could have originated in Jewish Christian sources. This expression encapsulates the claim that Muhammad definitively interprets

---

35 Cf. Colpe 2006, p. 210.
36 Roncaglia 1971, p. 105.
37 It has been suggested that the "Sabeans" mentioned in the Qur'an should be thought of as an "Anabaptist sect after the manner of the Mandaeans in the south of Iraq" (Maier, Bernhard: Koranlexikon [Qur'an Lexicon]. Kröner: Stuttgart 2001, p. 145) who, like Muslims, Jews and Christians "believed in God and the Last Day" (cf. Suras 2:62 and 5:69).
38 Sura 33:40: "Muhammad is not the father of [any] one of your men, but [he is] the Messenger of Allāh and seal [i.e. last] of the prophets. And ever is Allāh, of all things, Knowing."

and provides a fitting climax to all previous prophetic messages and thus "seals" them. A possible source text for this concept of theological finality is the New Testament Letter to the Hebrews, which addresses various Jewish Christian questions. This letter begins as follows: "In times past, God spoke in partial and various ways to our ancestors through the prophets; in these last days, he spoke to us through a *son*." (Hebr 1:1–2). So, even if the concept of a final seal on previous traditions could also have Manichaean origins,[39] it bears–as is clear from the quotation from the Letter to the Hebrews–a Jewish Christian stamp. In any event, the idea of a final seal on previous revelations is not a Qur'anic novelty.

It should also be noted that the dependence on the sources is often not so much directly textual, but rather a "forma mentis" or mindset which has Semitic or, even more probably, Jewish Christian roots.[40]

Another Jewish Christian motif found in the Qur'an is that of the Word of God being conveyed through the agency of an angel.[41] Undoubtedly of biblical origin (cf., for example, the Annunciation in Lk 1), this motif has also left its traces in Jewish

---

39 Cf. Roncaglia 1971, p. 108.
40 This lack of direct textual "evidence" for the term "Seal of the Prophet" in heretical Jewish Christian writings prompted Colpe to look for its origin in Manichaeism, where it is in fact to be found: "It is quite possible that Mani coined the term for himself, and that Muhammad adopted it. The presence of Manichaeans in his environment, from whom he might have come to know the term and felt challenged to competitively outdo it, is now well known." (Colpe 2006, p. 203 f.). Cf. section 1.3 on the Manichaean elements in the Qur'an.
41 Sura 5:48: "And We have revealed to you, [O Muhammad], the Book [i.e. the Qur'an] in truth, confirming that which preceded it of the Scripture and as a criterion over it."

Christianity as a similar idea is found in the Jewish Christian *Book of Elchasai* from the second century.[42] Another example is the motif of the expectation of a new Moses in the Qur'an. This expectation probably did not find its way into the Qur'an directly through the corresponding passage in Deuteronomy,[43] but rather through some form of Jewish Christian mediation, since this theological motif played a prominent role in Jewish Christian writings.

The accusation of the falsification of the scriptures

The Qur'anic doctrine of the "falsification of the Scriptures"–a frequent polemic in the Qur'an against Jews and Christians–most probably also has its origins in a Jewish Christian context or in the polemical disputes within Jewish Christianity.[44] For example, Bishop Epiphanius of Salamis (320–403) writes about the Jewish Christian Ebionites: "They allow the Gospel of Matthew, the only one they use, and which they call the Gospel of the Hebrews. This Gospel of Matthew, which they possess, is not complete, but falsified and mutilated."[45] It is interesting to note that there is mention of only *one* gospel here. This is also the case in the Qur'an, which never refers to *four* gospels, but only to the *one* gospel, in Arabic *Injil*. As in the Qur'an, the accusation of scriptural falsification, directed at adversaries, is also to be found in the Jewish Christian *pseudo-Clementine* homilies. Jewish

---

42 Cf. Hippolyte of Rome, *Elenchos* IX, 13–15; quoted in: Roncaglia 1971, p. 111.
43 Dt 18:15: "A prophet like me will the Lord your God, raise up for you from among your own kindred."
44 More on the anti-Jewish polemics of the Qur'an in Chapter 2 of this book.
45 Epiphanius, *Panarion* XXX, 3, 13. Quoted in: Roncaglia 1971, p. 121.

Christians and Muslims thus seemed to be in agreement about the "necessity to restore the Hebrew Scriptures."[46] Differences between various manuscripts may also have played a role in this dispute.

The question of the roots of this accusation is not only of historical interest. It is particularly explosive because this accusation of deliberate falsification of the content of the Scriptures is firmly entrenched in the Qur'an and therefore has consequences for the image that many Muslims have of Jews and Christians: "falsifiers of the Scriptures."

Identifiable sources

The Jewish Christian elements in the Qur'an are an indication that "the Muslim converts of the first hour came partly from these sectarian Ebionite circles. They drew their religious teachings from a rich literature."[47] A special role was played by the so-called *Kerygmata Petrou*, the so-called "Preaching of Peter" which feature the motif of an "expected prophet" as well as the characterization "of Adam as the first incarnation of the true prophet and as sinless".[48] There are also clear anti-Trinitarian elements in this work, as is often the case in the Qur'an as well. At the time, the boundaries between *Jewish* writings and those that could be termed more specifically Jewish Christian were still fluid, but anti-Trinitarian statements were present in both. Another borrowing from Jewish Christianity could also be the direction of prayer towards Jerusalem, to which the Jewish Christian leader Elchasai had committed his followers[49]–as did Muhammad during the early Medinan period.

---

46 Roncaglia 1971, p. 121 f.
47 Roncaglia 1971, p. 117.
48 Roncaglia 1971, p. 118.
49 Cf. Roncaglia 1971, p. 119.

The Islamic prohibition of wine may also be presumed to have Jewish Christian origin, since Elchasai prescribed the use of water instead of wine in the liturgy.[50]

The relevance of the question of Jewish Christian influences

The Jewish Christian groups which had existed for centuries up to the time of the origin of the Qur'an, have long since disappeared, crushed in the conflict between Judaism and Christianity, with their remnants absorbed into the emerging Islam. Christian groups claiming this heritage today are more likely to belong to the Evangelical spectrum.[51]

Jewish Christian influences on the Qur'an should not only be regarded as a matter of historical-literary analysis. The vital *theological* theme that emerges here is the dramatic loss of a common basis for interpreting the *identical* biblical narrative that Jews and Christians share. Jewish Christian sects of the first centuries made a desperate effort to bridge that gap. Their failure to achieve that goal provided a favorable milieu for the emergence of Islam. In this context, the Qur'an then used Jewish Christian sources for its own particular message.

The Jewish Christian elements preserved in the Qur'an raise two important theological questions for today: Would a new understanding between Christianity and Judaism also open up the possibility of "responding" *theologically* to the Qur'an and

---

50 Cf. Roncaglia 1971, p. 120.
51 Cf. the description of the Messianic Jews in: Kutschera, Rudolf: Das Heil kommt von den Juden (Joh 4,22). Untersuchungen zur Heilsbedeutung Israels [Salvation comes from the Jews (Jn 4:22). Studies on the salvific significance of Israel]. Peter Lang: Frankfurt a. M. 2003, pp. 323–340.

Islam? And related to this: Might not the conspicuous presence of Jewish Christian elements in the Qur'an be an incentive for Jews and Christians to increase their efforts to develop a common interpretation of their biblical heritage?

1.3 Manichaean elements

Manichaeism in the context of the emerging Islam

Manichaeism is characterized by a strict dualism as well as various Gnostic elements ("salvation through knowledge"). Evidence of Manichaean traces in the Qur'an should be sought less in direct text parallels than in the similarity of Qur'anic and Manichaean teachings. Its founder, Mani (216–276), had great influence both in the Western[52] and in the Eastern Roman Empire and beyond, that is, in the region where Islam would later emerge. Mani himself "grew up in the Jewish Christian Anabaptist community of the Elchasaites"[53] and transformed the Jewish Christian elements he encountered. His declared intention, entirely in the tradition of the Jewish Christians, was to restore "the true teaching."

While Manichaeism was extinguished in the course of the 6th century due to severe persecution by the Byzantine Empire, it continued in the (Persian) Sassanid Empire until its Islamization. Remnants of it remained alive in certain Central Asian regions even into the 16th century.[54]

---

52 The Church Father, St Augustine of Hippo (354–430), who lived more than a century after Mani, was a Manichaean for about ten years.

53 Entry on Mani/Manichäismus [Mani/Manichaeism]. In: Lexikon für Theologie und Kirche [Lexicon of Theology and the Church]. Volume 6. Herder: Freiburg 2009, p. 1266.

54 Cf. footnote 53, p. 1268 f.

Manichaean textual references in the Qur'an

Certain suras suggest that the Qur'anic authors were also aware of Manichaean teachings.[55] It is typical of Manichaeism that there was nothing like a doctrinal prototype which could be handed down as a rigid principle. Accordingly, Manichaeism can only be adequately "understood by examining its *process of becoming*, which is related to Mani's system of thought, which was always in a state of emergence and change. It is this tendency to adopt new ideas and perfect them that makes Mani and Muhammad justifiably comparable in the history of religion. For in this respect, they have a true spiritual affinity."[56]

The Islamic scholar R. Simon therefore emphasizes above all the structural similarity of these two religions: "They are also comparable with each other in so far as they claim to embrace all earlier religions and to be their culmination and apogee."[57] So it is not so much textual similarities that are important here but the extraordinary "ability to combine" which these two religions share. In the development of Muhammad's faith, one can observe the change from a more ascetic, world-denying first Mecca phase to a more world-affirming attitude in Medina. The Medina phase, in which he had to organize the practical aspects of a community, gave rise to his firm rejection of world-denial.[58]

---

55 While an active presence on the Arabian Peninsula is difficult to prove, Manichaeism radiated from Mesopotamia to this region and was particularly popular among traders (cf. footnote 13: Simon 1997, p. 132).

56 Simon 1997, p. 125.

57 Simon 1997, p. 125.

58 Cf. Sura 6:76–79.

Convergence and divergence in content

Apart from this structural similarity, there are also convergences in *content* between Manichaeism and Islam.[59] The most striking is the idea in both religions that in the beginning "there was only *one* authentic and universal religion, which due to various problems was either falsified or fragmented into sects."[60] The doctrine of the falsification of the original religion, and the impetus to restore this original religion, are further parallels between Manichaeism and Islam. Accordingly, both Manichaeism and Islam see themselves as universal religions to be spread by missionary activity. A quotation of Mani's has been preserved which could just as well have come from Muhammad: "The original religions were in one country and in one language. But my religion is such that it will be manifest in every country and in every language and will be taught in far-off lands."[61] Somewhat analogous to this universal claim in Manichaeism, is the designation of Islam in Sura 30:30 as a singular source of religion: "So direct your face [i.e. yourself] toward the religion, inclining to truth. [Adhere to] the fitrah of Allāh upon which He has created [all] people. No change should there be in the creation of Allāh. That is the correct religion."

A further parallel is the Manichaean doctrine of the series of prophets, similar to that in Jewish Christianity, culminating in

---

59 The fact that Róbert Simon argues cautiously in his investigation makes his results all the more credible. He also lists precisely the substantive differences, such as (Manichaean) dualism versus (Islamic) strict monotheism, the Islamic idea of the creation of the world by God/Allāh, whereas this idea has no place in Manichaeism since it considers the world to be evil and thus to be rejected. Cf. Simon 1997, p. 127 f.
60 Simon 1997, p. 133.
61 Quoted by: Simon 1997, p. 134.

Mani himself, who saw himself as the "Seal of the Prophets", as was the case with Muhammad in Islam.[62] In short, Manichaeism provided essential categories of thought on the basis of which the emerging Islam could develop its own teachings.

However, there is also an essential difference between them: the Islamic concept of jihad as a means of disseminating its teachings was unknown in Manichaeism. The appropriation of foreign religious ideas and their transformation into a powerful political-military-religious ideology is therefore a novelty unique to Islam.

1.4 Further influences on the Qur'an and emerging Islam

The unity of politics and religion in the Byzantine Empire

In the face of the threatening collapse of the Roman Empire, Emperor Constantine (272–337) had already discovered the unifying potential of the Christian church and incorporated it into his politics.[63] He thus convened the First Council of Nicaea (325). In doing so, Emperor Constantine was not primarily influenced by specific theological motives but rather, in addition to pragmatic political considerations ("How can imperial unity be preserved?"), by Neo-Platonic thinking on unity.

---

62 Cf. the corresponding references in Simon 1997, p. 136.
63 Section 1.4 owes much to the contribution of Arnold Stötzel in: Verstehen der jüdisch-christlichen Offenbarung ansgesichts des Islam [Understanding Jewish Christian revelation in the face of Islam]. In: Heute in Kirche und Welt 1/2002 and 2/2002. Bad Tölz 2002, pp. 4–5.

This paved the way for the idea of the unity of the state and the Christian church, which was later to find its full expression in the Byzantine Empire, embodied in the Eastern Roman Emperor Justinian I (482–565). He is considered the architect of the state church in Byzantium, which meant that, from a theological point of view, the emperor could consider himself to be God's representative on earth. However, any opposition to this idea of unity of State and Church was mercilessly repressed. So, for example, the construction of the Hagia Sophia in Constantinople, initiated by Justinian, was preceded by the suppression of the so-called Nika uprising in 532, in which about 30,000 people were massacred on the emperor's order. It could thus be said that fervent religiosity and cold terror existed cheek by jowl.

It must be said that this unity of State and religion was the norm for all ancient forms of government. The novelty in the Byzantine context was the extension of this concept to Christianity which had certainly not been conceived as a "State religion," as the life and teachings of Jesus amply show.

In the year 570, five years after the death of Justinian, Muhammad was born. It was presumably during his extensive trade journeys that Muhammad came into contact with the Byzantine Empire and its identity shaped by the unity of State and religion, and was influenced by it.

Theological divisions within Christianity

Islam came into being exactly at a time of dramatic doctrinal disputes within Christianity and their subsequent clarifications. These disputes related mainly to the Monophysite and Nestorian trends in Christianity, which had been condemned at the Councils of Ephesus (431) and Chalcedon (451) and eventually split from mainstream Christianity. These councils, like those of Nicaea (325) and Constantinople (381) before them, considered some fundamental questions of the Christian faith: How could the Jewish confession of faith in the one God be preserved and, at the same time, the innovations introduced by the New Testament through the person of Jesus Christ be understood and embraced?

The clarifications that gradually emerged brought with them distinctions and separations. This also had political consequences, since any dissenter from the emperor's faith was not only considered a heretic or a schismatic, but also an enemy of the Empire. Such forced unity of Church and State led to ever new tensions in the Empire and increased the desire for independence. Christians who refused to submit to this coercion emigrated, seeking the protection of the Persians outside the Roman Empire or undertaking missionary work on the Arabian Peninsula. Syria, Palestine and Egypt, which favored a break with Byzantium of which they were a part, later saw in Islam a welcome liberator. At this time a Jacobite church in Syria and a Nestorian church in Persia emerged, in addition to an Armenian church, which had already been formed at the beginning of the 4th century.

This situation of a torn Church forms the backdrop to the Qur'anic interpretation of the divisions within Christianity in Sura 5:14: "And from those who say, 'We are Christians' We [= Allāh] took their covenant; but they forgot a portion of that of which they were reminded. So We caused among them animosity and hatred until the Day of Resurrection." What the Qur'an is saying here is that the discord that broke out among the Christians is due to their disloyalty to the message of Jesus. Sura 3:105 holds this situation up to Muslims as a deterrent: "And do not be like the ones who became divided and differed after the clear proofs had come to them."

The idea that the struggle to arrive at the truth might be a process lasting centuries had no traction here. The loss of the unity of faith–in fact a tragedy within Christianity up to the present day–is in this view a confirmation of Muslim claims.

Among the heretical doctrines that emerged in the early centuries of Christianity, triggered by the question of the nature of Jesus Christ, was Nestorianism. Nestorius (386–451), Patriarch of Constantinople, was convinced–as affirmed by the Councils of Ephesus (431) and Chalcedon (451)–that Jesus indeed had two natures, the human and the divine, but that, contrary to the position taken by the two councils, these were not united in one person and one "substance." Thus Nestorius taught that Jesus is "the person accepted by the Logos, in whom he dwells as in a temple."[64]

How does this doctrine relate to Qur'anic thought?

Theological analogies between Islam and Nestorianism

Although the direct dependence of the Qur'an on Nestorian sources (an accusation often leveled by Christian theologians) is difficult to prove, there are astonishing analogies in content. This starts with the rejection of the doctrinal positions adopted by the Councils of Ephesus (431) and Chalcedon (451) by both the Nestorians and emerging Islam.

In the year 612, at about the same time that Muhammad experienced his "vocational call" (in the year 610), the Persian King Chosroes II met with the Christian Nestorian bishops and

---

64 This formula used by Nestorius (381–451) is typical of the "Antiochene School," of which he was part before becoming Patriarch of Constantinople (428–431); quoted in: Nestorius/Nestorianismus [Nestorius/Nestorianism]. In: Lexikon für Theologie und Kirche. Vol. 7 Herder: Freiburg 2009, p. 747. The Nestorian churches still existing today confess the Christology of Nestorius in the formula: "two natures, two hypostases, one person in Christ." (In: Lexikon für Theologie und Kirche, ibid.).

monks of his country for a religious discussion. The Persians, in a sense the hereditary enemies of Byzantium, had become the patrons of the Nestorians. The meeting was called to discuss questions such as "Did the Nestorians deviate from the foundations of their faith?" and "Did Mary give birth to Christ or to God?" The Nestorian response begins with an emphatic confession of the uniqueness of God:

"We believe in a divine entity. It is eternal, without beginning. Alive, all animating. Powerful, creating all powers. Pure spirit. Infinite, incomprehensible. Not put together and without parts. Incorporeal. Invisible and unchanging. Unable to suffer and immortal. Neither through them [= the divine being] nor through others nor with others can suffering and change occur."[65]

Although such a text could just as well have been written by Byzantine, that is, Orthodox authors, it is striking that the emphasis on monotheism is accompanied by a certain rigidity. In any case, it was inconceivable for the Nestorians that the "Logos of God" could also *become* a human being, that is, that God could become a participant in real historical events. When the Nestorian bishops defend monotheism, they use the Syrian word "Allāh" for "God." At the turn of the 6th century, thus during the Muhammad's lifetime, a Nestorian theologian summarized the theological position of Nestorianism as follows: "The Messiah, Marjam's son, is not God/Allāh. If Mary is the mother of a man, then she is not, she cannot be the mother of God."[66]

---

[65] Quoted from: Abramomowski, Luise et al (Eds.): A Nestorian Collection of Christological Texts. Volume I, Syriac Text; Volume II, Introduction, Translation and Indexes. Cambridge University Press: Cambridge, 1972, here: A Nestorian Collection I, p. 150 f. (original text), II, p. 88 f. (English translation).

[66] Quoted from: A Nestorian Collection II (cf. footnote 65), p. XXXIV.

Sura 5:17 expresses an analogous view to that of the Nestorians: "They have certainly disbelieved who say that Allāh is Christ, the son of Mary. Say, 'Then who could prevent Allāh at all if He had intended to destroy Christ, the son of Mary, or his mother or everyone on the earth?' And to Allāh belongs the dominion of the heavens and the earth and whatever is between them. He creates what He wills, and Allāh is over all things competent."

It is inconceivable that the Allāh represented in this way could enter into history with human beings as true *partners*, and consequently, he cannot tolerate any "son of man" alongside himself. Repeatedly, therefore, the Qur'an sharply rejects the Christian image of God, for example in Sura 5:72: "Indeed, he who associates others with Allāh–Allāh has forbidden him Paradise, and his refuge is the Fire. And there are not for the wrongdoers any helpers."

In contrast to Western Christianity, neither Islam nor Nestorianism succeeded in formulating the concept of personhood. Centuries of theological reflection on the nature of Jesus on the part of the Church led to this concept and the dignity of man associated with it. This concept is eloquently summarized in an old liturgical daily prayer for Christmas: "O God, who wonderfully created the dignity of human nature and still more wonderfully restored it, grant, we pray, that we may share in the divinity of Christ, who humbled himself to share in our humanity."

Influences of ancient Roman legal thought

As was the case with Nestorianism as outlined above, there is also no evidence that Islam was *directly* influenced by ancient Roman legal thought. There are, however, convergences in content, as can be seen in the claim to universality and the regulations on war and peace.[67]

The universal claim to power in ancient Roman thought is exemplified in a statement by the Roman politician and philosopher Marcus Tullius Cicero (106–43 B.C.): "There is in fact a law namely right reason, which is in accordance with nature, applies to all men and is unchangeable and eternal ... It will not lay down one rule at Rome and another at Athens, nor will it be one rule today and another tomorrow. But there will be one law eternal and unchangeable binding all times and upon all peoples."[68]

Similarly, in Islam, the whole world is the domain of Allāh. This becomes evident in Sura 2:107, for example, in the form of a rhetorical question: "Do you not know that to Allāh belongs the dominion of the heavens and the earth and [that] you have not besides Allāh any protector or any helper?" For the individual Muslim as well as for an Islamic state, to be in the service of Allāh *can* therefore mean nothing other than to recognize this world dominion and to promote its spread. After the defeat at the Battle of Tours (732), early Islamic legal scholars came to the insight that the world is divided into two areas: dār al-Islām (the house or abode of Islam) on the one hand, and dār al-ḥarb (the house or abode of war) on the other hand. The "House of Islam" refers to the territory under Muslim rule where the members of the tolerated religions (the dhimmīs) pay the head tax (jizya).[69] The "House of War" includes all areas outside

---

67 The following remarks are essentially based on the long-standing research on Islamic law by Majid Khadduri (1909–2007), especially on the subject of war and peace: Khadduri, Majid: War and Peace in the Law of Islam. The Lawbook Exchange: Clark/New Jersey 2006.
68 Quoted by Khadduri 2006, p. X.
69 Cf. Sura 9:29: "Fight those who do not believe in Allāh or in the Last Day and who do not consider unlawful what Allāh and His

Islamic-dominated territory. From this perspective, the "House of Islam" is, inevitably, always in conflict with the "House of War," because the latter, by its very existence, contradicts the claim to the recognition of the worldwide dominion of Allāh.

This leads logically to the acceptance of the *necessity* of struggle. On the political level, the religiously based "Jihad" against the "House of War" is consequently the regular instrument used by Islamic states to transform the whole world into the "House of Peace." However, for purely practical reasons, this is not always possible, which is why there are also phases of non-warfare.[70]

Jihad, which literally means "exerted effort," is an ambiguous term. Islamic jurists therefore apply the term Jihad to four areas of activity, namely "by his heart; his tongue; his hands; and by the sword. The first is concerned with combating the devil and in the attempt to escape his persuasion to evil. This type of jihad, so significant in the eyes of the Prophet Muhammad, was regarded as the greater jihad. The second and third are mainly fulfilled in supporting the right and correcting the wrong. The fourth is precisely equivalent to the meaning of war, and is concerned with fighting the unbelievers and the enemies of the faith. The

---

Messenger have made unlawful and who do not adopt the religion of truth [i.e. Islam] from those who were given the Scripture–[fight] until they give the jizyah willingly while they are humbled." For the historical circumstances of this provision, cf. section 2.3: Phases in the Relationship with the Jews.

70 However, these intervals, in which legally regulated methods, above all negotiations and peace treaties, are applied, must not exceed 10 years. If after 10 years that the resumption of regular warfare is not feasible, then a further 10-year ceasefire period is declared.

believers are under obligation of sacrificing their wealth and lives in the prosecution of war."[71]

Naturally, the *collective* obligation to undertake the jihad of war is not necessarily incumbent on *all* believers. This is neither possible nor desirable for purely practical reasons. At the same time, however, the consequence of this *collective* obligation is that the responsibility for deciding whether and when such a war jihad is declared, rests on the state-religious authorities. Generally, the following principle applies: "The existence of a dār al-harb ["war zone", i.e. a part of the world ruled by non-Muslims] is ultimately outlawed under the Islamic jural order [...], the dār al-Islām [the Muslim ruled part of the world] is permanently under jihād obligation until the dār al-harb is reduced to non-existence [...]. The universalism of Islam, in its all-embracing creed, is imposed on the believers as a continuous process of warfare, psychological and political if not explicitly military."[72] This fundamental state can be suspended, but it can also be proclaimed anew at any time. Drawing on numerous sources, Khaddouri therefore concludes that Muslim jurists, like their Roman forefathers, followed the principle: "*Si vis pacem, para bellum*" (If you want peace, prepare for war).

If you ask where the concept of a holy war comes from in this context, you will find a striking parallel to Roman legal thinking. For both in Islam and in ancient Rome, "not only was war to be *justum* [=just], but also to be *pium* [=holy], that is, in accordance with the sanction of religion and the implied commands of gods."[73] The claim to universality and the idea of "holy war" ("bellum pium") were thus already present in

---

71 Khadduri 2006, p. 56 f. The obligation of sacrificing "wealth and lives" refers to Sura 61:11.

72 Khadduri 2006, p. 64.

73 Khadduri 2006, p. 57.

Roman thought in antiquity. These forms of thought would also be incorporated into the Qur'an–as they were indeed–as a text of late antiquity and thus become part of the emerging Islam.

So what did the Qur'an make of all these sources and what is the uniquely Muslim character of this book?

1.5 The specific Islamic accent

Traditional judgments of Christian theologians on the Qur'an

In the course of the history of Christian theology, the image of the Qur'an was for centuries shaped by a comparison with the Bible and Christian dogma. For example, John Damascene (ca. 650–750)–who lived at the time of the Qur'an's emergence–describes Islam "as the last of the ancient church heresies."[74] Thomas Aquinas (1225–1274), in his *Summa contra Gentiles* (Book I, Chapter 6), accuses Muhammad of mixing basic truth with fable and false doctrine. Nikolaus Cusanus (1401–1464), in his *Cribratio Alkorani* ("A Scrutiny of the Koran"), seven years after the fall of Constantinople, made an attempt "to 'sift' and 'sieve' the Qur'an for its biblical content with a view to branding Islam as Christian heresy."[75] In the course of the so-called "Basel Qur'an Controversy" in 1543, which concerned the first printed Latin version of the Qur'an, the Protestant editor and promoter of this work, Theodore Bibliander (1505–1564), took the view that "basically nothing new is taught in

---

74 Maier 2001, p. 95.
75 Maier 2001, p. 126.

the Quran: everything had already been represented among the Christian heretics."[76]

These assessments view the Qur'an as misguided text with Christian origins, some even regarding it as *plagiarism* pure and simple. In the ancient world, the appropriation of existing authoritative texts was not yet frowned upon, and was certainly not considered intellectual property theft as it is today.[77]

However, it must be said that the mere reproduction of existing sources *alone* would not have made Islam what it is today. That is why an attempt must now be made to pinpoint what it is that is uniquely Islamic about the Qur'an. In other words: what specifically Islamic value has been added to the Qur'an which distinguishes it from its sources?

The combination of poetry and a sense of superiority

The western reader is frequently unaware of the exceptional *cultural* significance of the Qur'an which occupies a unique position within the Arabic language and Arab culture. The Qur'an is *the* crowning achievement of Arabic literature and *the* pinnacle of Arabic poetry, and thus to this day their primary point of reference. In particular, the sound and poetic quality of the suras often send the Arabic-speaking reader or listener into a kind of rapture, making them intensely aware of the presence of Allāh in these moments. The recitation of the Qur'an is

---

76 Martin Wallraff, *Vorwort* [Preface], p. X, in: Neuwirth, Angelika: Koranforschung–eine politische Philologie? [Qur'anic Studies–a Political Philology?]. De Gruyter: Berlin 2014.

77 This term is controversial in contemporary Islamic studies, not least because it is associated with the accusation that the Qur'an has contributed nothing unique, or specifically Islamic, to the identified sources. That is why section 1.5 specifically seeks to evaluate this contribution.

often also accompanied by a sense of intoxicating superiority, because its content always suggests that, in contrast to previous traditions, Islam is in complete possession of divine truth ("Seal of the Prophets"). The aesthetic-cultural-religious experience thus merges with the content, and it is precisely this merging that is a central characteristic of the Qur'an.

The specifically Islamic theological emphasis

In addition to cultural and psychological aspects, there are also theological aspects to be considered: The novelty of the Islamic *content* lies above all in its theological simplification and schematization of the preceding traditions and influences.

This is illustrated, for example, in Sura 112, which under the title "Purification" (i.e. purification of faith) summarizes the Qur'anic image of God as follows:

"1. Say, 'He is Allāh, [who is] One,
2. Allāh, the Eternal Refuge.
3. He neither begets nor is born (other translation: Neither begetting nor begotten),
4. Nor is there to Him any equivalent.'"

Analysis of the original Arabic text shows[78] that verse 1 is a free translation of the *Sh'ma Israel*, the Jewish confession of faith.[79] The close association with the biblical text is evident from the use of the Arabic word *aḥad* ("one"; in Hebrew *eḥad*), the use of

---

78 In what follows: cf. Neuwirth 2019, pp. 477–482.
79 The beginning of this prayer reads in the original biblical text as follows: "Hear O Israel! The LORD is our God, the LORD alone! Therefore you shall love the LORD, your God, with your whole heart, and with your whole being, and with your whole strength" (Deuteronomy 6:4–5).

which is "a violation of Arabic grammar."[80] The original address to Israel is taken up here *and* at the same time changed. Thus, the biblical Jewish basic credo, the familiarity of which could be assumed, becomes a universal text in Sura 112:1, since to "make the Jewish credo universally valid, and thus also acceptable to non-Jewish hearers, the text is reformulated, but without losing the distinct form in which it already possesses authority."[81]

At the same time, however, this sura also refers to the Nicene Creed, where Christ is defined as "begotten, not made." Sura 112:3 both echoes and rejects this statement, using a doubly negative formulation which is just as emphatic as its counterpart in the Nicene Creed. This formulation deliberately and skillfully overturns the original text and proceeds to the logical conclusion summarized in Sura 112:4: "And no one is like him." In the original Arabic text, the word used for "equal" is *kufuwan*, a word used just this once in the Qur'an, and is a deliberate contrast to the "homoousios" of the Nicene Creed, which signifies that Christ is consubstantial with God, the Father. The reason for the formulation in Sura 112:3 was the desire of the first Muslim community in Medina to break through to its Jewish audience. The hope was that, by reformulating the Jewish confession of faith in the one God, while simultaneously rejecting Christological interpretations of the concept, Jewish converts would be won over to the new Muslim faith.

This short analysis highlights the genuinely new aspect of the Qur'an. It appropriated certain Jewish and Christian beliefs, using them as a foil to its own claims to superiority, and reworked them into a new religious-poetic text which appealed in particular to a target audience that considered its

---

[80] Neuwirth 2019, p. 479.
[81] Neuwirth 2019, p. 479.

Jewish and Christian antecedents as having been surpassed. In other words: in line with the post-biblical syncretism that was widespread in the Arab world at the time, the existing sources were assimilated, fragmented and reassembled as the basis for a comprehensive politico-religious system. Reflecting a trend towards universality that had already emerged in Roman antiquity, the Qur'an thus became a starting point for a project that began with the conquest of Mecca during Muhammad's lifetime and led to the worldwide expansion of Islam after his death: "The founding of a religious state in stateless Arabia, the unification of the Arabs for a project of world conquest–*that* is what is really new about Islam."[82] Over all this towers the figure of Allāh, who can best be characterized as Muhammad's "alter ego" [= the other side of himself].

This logic of superiority and universalization is the foundation of Islam to this day: the whole world and the life of each individual must be made to conform to this *God-given order (ad-dīn)*.[83] This order, based on the Qur'an, encompasses *everything* from the individual behavior and faith of every single Muslim to a hoped-for new world order. Maps of the early Islamic conquests illustrate the military impact of that dynamic.[84]

---

[82] Ammann, Ludwig: Der altarabische weltanschauliche und religiöse Kontext des Korans [The Old Arabic ideological and religious context of the Qur'an]. In: Hartwig 2008, p. 231.

[83] The Islamic scholar Tilman Nagel, for example, explains what this means in terms of the individual non-Muslim: "For every human being who is formed by Allāh in the womb has this creative bond with Allāh, the fitra, which no one can change (Sura 30:30). Even if parents are "misguided" and educate their child to another religion [e.g. Christianity], this core is not touched by it." (Nagel 2018, p. 33).

[84] Cf., for example: https://www.olivetree.com/blog/learned-love-church-history/spread-islam/ (accessed on 25/04/2020).

How the Qur'an uses the biblical models it discovered, transforming and incorporating them into a new belief system, will be examined further by considering the question of Anti-Judaism in the Qur'an.

2. Anti-Judaism in the Qur'an?

2.1 The seriousness of the question

Two current examples

Anti-Judaism in the Qur'an is not only a historical issue–it remains relevant today, as the following examples illustrate.

In the memoir of her childhood in the Arab-Muslim milieu of Canada published in 2019, the educator, author and human rights activist, Yasmine Mohammed, describes the "pervasive hate for Jewish people–and this is learned from a young age. In Muslim communities, the word for Jew is not only used as a pejorative, it is used as a curse word. It is a hate that permeates so much that it is invisible: It is just accepted. Never once, as a Muslim, did I stop to think about why we were to hate Jewish people so much ... It's like asking a child why they hate monsters. It is just a learned behavior that rarely gets questioned, and the hate of Israel is an extension of that."[85]

One of the numerous attempts to win Christians over to the anti-Jewish cause took place during Pope Benedict XVI's visit to Jerusalem on 11 May 2009. The chief Islamic judge of the Palestinian Authority, Sheikh Taysir Rajab, in the presence of the Pope, called on Christians to unite with Muslims against what he called the "murderous" Israelis, a thinly veiled reference to the Jews.[86]

---

85 From the online edition of the *Jerusalem Post* of 18.08.2018: *https://www.jpost.com/Middle-East/Ex-Muslim-to-Post-Trying-to-teach-naive-West-about-true-nature-of-Islam-598946* (accessed on 27/08/2019).

86 For more details on this infamous speech that the author witnessed in person, cf.: https://www.irishtimes.com/news/pope-leaves-function-after-cleric-s-attack-on-israel-1.762302 (accessed on 12/11/2019).

Are these isolated episodes that should be overlooked in the light of the many past manifestations of peaceful Muslim-Jewish coexistence? Or do they in fact highlight the need to go *beyond submission* and subject this issue to unflinching scrutiny?

The decisive question is: how does this very real Muslim Anti-Judaism[87] relate to the central text of Islam, the Qur'an? The facile response of referencing the Middle East conflict to justify such attitudes is clearly inadequate.

An illustrative Qur'anic verse

Sura 5:32, often cited as proof of Islam's love of peace[88], is an example of a manifestation of the problem, as it reads as follows: "[...] whoever kills a soul [...], it is as if he had slain mankind entirely. And whoever saves one [...], it is as if he had saved mankind entirely." The Qur'an puts this almost literal quotation from the Talmud[89] into the mouth of Allāh, with the verse introduced in the "we" form as follows: "Because of that, We decreed upon the Children of Israel that [...]". However, this quotation, which indeed reflects a high ethical standard, is neither an invitation to Muslims to renounce violence nor a tribute to Israel. Quite the contrary: Sura 5:32 should be read in the context of the numerous admonitions to the "children

---

87 We are dealing here with *Anti-Judaism* rather than *anti-Semitism*. The latter term would be inappropriate since, according to biblical genealogy, Noah's son Sem is also the progenitor of the Arabs.

88 For example, in statements by Islamic associations following the Paris attacks in 2015.

89 Cf. Sanhedrin 37a-37b in The William Davidson Talmud: digital edition of the Babylonian Talmud. Translated by Rabbi Adin Even-Israel Steinsaltz. https://www.sefaria.org/Sanhedrin.37b?lang=bi (accessed on 17/11/2019).

of Israel," that is to say, the Jews. Therefore, it is immediately followed by a grim announcement in Sura 5:33: "Indeed, the penalty for those who wage war against Allāh and His Messenger and strive upon earth [to cause] corruption is none but that they be killed or crucified or that their hands and feet be cut off from opposite sides."

How do such statements come about?

The transformation of biblical content in the Qur'an

At the time the Qur'an[90] came into being in the 7th/8th century CE, the Arabian Peninsula was characterized by a wide variety of cultures and religions. Muhammad himself, and the community he had gathered around him, were well aware of them. They were also aware of the numerous conflicts within this religious-cultural mix.

The Qur'an is therefore an agglomeration of widely differing texts, oral traditions and the polemics of the time, and also includes many biblical narratives and motifs. However, since the authors of the Qur'an did not normally have the written biblical texts at their disposal, what they recorded was mainly what had been transmitted orally, often influenced by Jewish or Christian interpretations. The biblical content and its interpretations were transformed by Muhammad and the Qur'anic authors with one specific intention: to endow the "prophet" and the emerging Muslim community with biblical authority. Accordingly, all the biblical figures in the Qur'an display some of Muhammad's own traits and at the same time reflect the state of discussion of topical issues in the early Muslim community.

Biblical figures in the Qur'an were often modelled in deliberate contrast to their Jewish and Christian roles. However, there must

---

90 Cf. section 1.1 The Qur'an in its historical context.

always be a careful examination of whether what Muhammad and the Qur'an authors perceived as typically Jewish or Christian is actually Jewish or Christian! Moreover, biblical figures often appear in the Qur'an within polemical arguments, which also distorts their image and the statements attributed to them.

A good example of this is to be found in Sura 9:30 ff., where the Jews are accused of regarding *Uzair*, that is, the biblical Ezra, as the Son of God. This accusation reflects serious misunderstandings. Muhammad generally rejected any notion of a "Son of God," with the word "Son" signifying a real being (sexually) begotten by "God" with a woman. This is of course not the Christian conception of Jesus as "Son of God" either, nor is it a theological concept in Judaism. This accusation, based on misunderstandings, attributes to the Jews an error similar to that of which, from the Qur'anic perspective, Christians were allegedly guilty with regard to Jesus. The historical background to this accusation may be a Jewish sect which revered Ezra in a special way and which came to Muhammad's attention. More probable, according to the Qur'an scholar, Heribert Busse, is "that Muhammad, in the heat of debate, wanted to accuse the Jews of a heretical doctrine on a par with the heresy of the Christian doctrine that teaches the divine nature of Jesus. In doing so, he could take advantage of the high esteem granted Ezra in Judaism."[91]

The issue of Anti-Judaism should be seen in the larger context of the Qur'an's attitude to the followers of other religions, which is briefly discussed below.

---

91 Busse 1998, p. 57.

Statements in the Qur'an on the plurality of religions

The evaluations of other religions and their followers in the Qur'an are not consistent. In Suras 2 and 5, for example, the beliefs of Jews and Christians are given the endorsement "that their creed is identical with Islam and that they, like Muslims, have a right to salvation. On the other hand, the situation is different with the list in Sura 22. The overall tenor is negative; the differences that exist between them 'God will decide on the day of resurrection'."[92] The Qur'anic evaluation of other religions depends above all on the attitude of their adherents to Muhammad and his followers in the nascent Islamic community.

Adam represents the ideal state of mankind that needs to be restored. In the Qur'an, this biblical figure becomes the protagonist of an allegedly unitary primeval religion. He does not represent the human being taken from the soil (*adamah* in Hebrew), as in the biblical original. Instead, the Qur'anic Adam is presented as the founder of a single community (*umma*–a word derived from Hebrew), united in faith.[93] Since this unity was subsequently shattered, God repeatedly sent prophets (including Noah, Moses, Jesus and Muhammad himself) to restore it. This aim can only be achieved in the "House of Peace," in a world dominated by Islam, a world that has subjected itself to Allāh in the sense envisaged by Muhammad.

Sura 5:48 provides a further explanation for religious diversity: "Had Allāh willed, He would have made you one nation [united in religion], but [He intended] to test you in what

---

92 Busse 1998, p. 30. Busse is referring here to Sura 22:17 in which "those who have believed" are contrasted with the Jews, Sabaeans, Christians, Magians (= Zoroastrians) and polytheists.

93 Cf.: Sura 2:213, "Mankind was [of] one religion [before their deviation] (other translations: Mankind was one community)."

He has given you; so race to [all that is] good. To Allāh is your return all together, and He will [then] inform you concerning that over which you used to differ." Occasionally the Qur'an also justifies religious pluralism simply by referring to ethnic diversity: many peoples imply many religions. However, this view was controversial within Islam. In the Qur'an, contradictory statements can quite unexpectedly stand side by side by referring to the omnipotence of Allāh as, for instance, in 25:54: "And ever is your Lord competent."

Jews and Christians are regarded by the Qur'an as the "People of the Scripture" or the "People of the Book:" they share in the revelations of the heavenly primeval script, the "Preserved Slate" (Sura 85:22), elsewhere also called "Mother of the Book" (Suras 13:39 and 43:4).

The followers of the Mosaic religion appear under two names in the Qur'an, especially from the Medinan phase onward: "Children of Israel" and "Jews." This distinction is above all determined by Jewish attitudes towards Jesus. The split between Judaism and Christianity has therefore shaped the Qur'anic attitude towards the Jews, with Christian Anti-Judaism seeping into the Qur'an. "According to the Qur'an, the Jews were nothing more than unbelieving Israelites: Jesus addressed the Children of Israel; these were divided into two groups, the Christians (naṣārā), who believed in Jesus, and the others, who were unbelievers. The latter were henceforth called Jews."[94]

The way in which the adherents of other religions were dealt with evolved over the course of Muhammad's lifetime. As will be shown in greater detail when considering the phases of Muhammad's relationship with the Jews, towards the end of his life Jews and Christians were tolerated under certain conditions.

---

94 Busse 1998, p. 31 f.

Polytheists, on the other hand, are often called those who "have attributed to Allāh: *partners*"–a term which can also be directed against Christians and their doctrine of the Trinity. They must in principle convert to Islam, because "The right course has become clear from the wrong" (Sura 2:256). They are granted a time limit within which to do this, at the end of which the Qur'an exhorts Muslims to act as follows: "And when the sacred months have passed, then kill the polytheists wherever you find them and capture them and besiege them and sit in wait for them at every place of ambush. But if they should repent, establish prayer, and give zakah, let them [go] on their way. Indeed, Allāh is Forgiving and Merciful." (Sura 9:5).

The theological motives underlying the Qur'an's attitude towards the Jews are particularly evident in the portrayal of two central figures of the biblical history of salvation: Abraham and Moses.

2.2 Abraham and Moses in the Qur'an

From the biblical Abraham
to the prototype of the pious Muslim

Despite the evocative expression "Abrahamic religions," the Qur'anic *Ibrahim*–referred to in several suras–apart from the name, bears hardly any resemblance to the biblical patriarch of Israel. This difference is first and foremost reflected in the omissions in the Qur'anic account as compared to the biblical narrative. In the Qur'an, "Abraham [...] never occurs as the progenitor of the Israelites"[95] *in the sense of being the depositary of a promise and responsible for its onward transmission to*

---

95 Neuwirth 2019, p. 394.

succeeding generations–the consistent biblical view in both Old and New Testaments.

Sura 2:124 goes one step further. In a conversation with Ibrahim, Allāh disinherited the allegedly iniquitous Israel to which Ibrahim refers as *my descendants*: "When Abraham was tried by his Lord with commands and he fulfilled them. [Allāh] said, 'Indeed, I will make you a leader for the people.' [Abraham] said, 'And of my descendants?' [Allāh] said, 'My covenant does not include the wrongdoers'."

However, the biblical promise to the Israelites, the descendants of Abraham, reads as follows: "All the families of the earth will find blessing in you" (Gen 12:3). The Qur'an has thus significantly modified the biblical narrative. It acknowledges Abraham, but in the same breath excludes Israel from the salvific tradition. This is reminiscent of anti-Jewish attitudes, as manifested throughout the course of church history. It is often hard to determine exactly *how* these Christian anti-Jewish attitudes, which historically preceded the Qur'an, influenced the Qur'anic text. However, distinct forms of Anti-Judaism have found their way into the Qur'an or have been generated by it– like the distorted portrayal of Abraham.

The desire of the emerging Muslim community to define its identity in relation to Abraham, while at the same time disparaging Jewish traditions, is also reflected in the Qur'an's depiction of the antagonism between Isaac and Ishmael. The biblical narrative of the "binding of Isaac" (Gen 22:1–19) reveals Abraham's unconditional trust in God. This enables God to fulfil his promise of blessing and it is precisely through this that Isaac learns how to believe. The Qur'an, however, turns this narrative into a mere father-son cultic act (cf. Sura 37:99–109) which then forms the basis of a sacrificial practice that continues to this day.[96]

---

96 One of the prescribed central elements of the pilgrimage to Mecca (the *Hajj*) is a commemoration and imitation of this aspect of

The Qur'anic version of the Abraham narrative also replaces the biblical bearer of the promise, Isaac, with Ishmael. Thus Sura 2:127 has Abraham and Ishmael building the sanctuary in Mecca–evidently without any biblical reference: "'And [mention] when Abraham was raising the foundations of the House and [with him] Ishmael, [saying], 'Our lord, accept [this] from us'." This act usurps biblical authority, which by rights rests with Jerusalem, and confers it on Mecca, as Sura 3:96–97 makes clear: "Indeed, the first House [of worship] established for mankind was that at Makkah–blessed and a guidance for the worlds. In it are clear signs [such as] the standing place of Abraham. And whoever enters it shall be safe."[97]

Thus Abraham is plucked from the Jewish and Christian traditions which, of course, historically precede the Qur'an, to become instead the precursor of Muhammad, as can be seen in Sura 3:65–68. There Muhammad presents his own claim to overcoming the Jewish Christian divide: "O People of the Scripture, why do you argue about Abraham while the Torah and the Gospel were not revealed until after him? Then will you not reason? ... Allāh knows, while you know not. Abraham was neither a Jew nor a Christian, but he was one inclining toward truth, a Muslim [submitting to Allāh]. And he was not of the

---

Abraham's personal history: "The pilgrims, following the example of Abraham, carry out his (intended) act of sacrifice. The sacrifice of Abraham, the Islamic Feast Sacrifice, *aḍḥā*, which pre-figures, so to speak, the obligatory slaughter of a sacrificial animal for every Meccan pilgrim, has become a ubiquitous object of popular pictorial representations." (Neuwirth 2014, p. 103). Abraham thus becomes the de facto founder of Meccan rites (cf. Sura 22:26 f.).

97 There are indications that Mecca was already connected with the Abraham narratives in the pre-Islamic period. In a sense, the Qur'an turned these pre-Islamic legendary traditions into a content of faith.

polytheists. Indeed, the worthiest of Abraham among the people are those who followed him [in submission to Allāh] and this prophet, and those who believe [in his message]. And Allāh is the ally of the believers."

The Arabic term used here for Abraham, ḥanīf, characterizes him as a "pre-denominational monotheist,"[98] i.e. an exemplary pious man before and beyond Judaism or Christianity. In some translations of the Qur'an, this Arabic word is simply rendered as "Muslim."[99] Abraham-Ibrahim thus becomes both the prototype of Muslims, al-muslimūn (cf. Sura 2:135 f.) and the mirror image of Muhammad. A grouping of Judaism, Christianity and Islam under the heading "Abrahamic religions" is thus excluded by the Qur'an itself.

The merging of Abraham and Muhammad–while excluding Israel–penetrates to the core of Muslim piety. The daily prayer of Muslims contains a formula that unites Abraham and Muhammad:

> "O Allāh, bless Muhammad and the members of his household as Thou didst bless the members of Ibrahim's household. Grant favors to Muhammad and the members of his household as Thou didst grant favors to the members of the household of Ibrahim in the world. Thou art indeed Praiseworthy and Glorious. "[100]

---

98 Neuwirth 2014, p. 106.
99 For example, in the *Sahih International Translation* cited above, and in the *Tarif Khalidi Translation* for Penguin Classics, 2009.
100 From *Kitab Al-Salat* (The Book of Prayers), Translation of Sahih Muslim, on: http://www.iium.edu.my/deed/hadith/muslim/004_smt.html (accessed on 17/11/2019).

Moses–from biblical lawgiver to Qur'anic accuser of the Jews

What is particularly striking about the Qur'anic version of the Moses (in Arabic, Musa) story, is how various biblical narratives were interwoven. Sura 28:38 says first of all about Pharaoh–as in the biblical account–that he opposes Moses and his plans. Then, in the same verse, Pharaoh instructs his Minister as follows: "Then ignite for me, O Haman, [a fire] upon the clay and make for me a tower that I may look at the God of Moses. And indeed, I do think he is among the liars." *Haman*, the anti-Jewish government official of the Persian king Xerxes from the biblical story of Esther, is thus conflated with Pharaoh and the Tower of Babel (from the book of Genesis) into a single story.

The Qur'anic figure of Moses/Musa reflects the different phases of Muhammad's life-story even more clearly than Abraham-Ibrahim. The Qur'an illustrates through the figure of Moses how one becomes a great prophet. The key stages in this process can be summarized as follows: "[...] the spiritual movement toward the transcendent God, the feeling of insufficient strength in the face of the task, the ambivalence between the obligation to familial lineage and the necessity of breaking with it, the experiencing of fear and overcoming it, and the power for patient persistence in a situation of humiliation."[101]

As already observed in the case of Abraham/Ibrahim, the omissions from the Moses-Musa narrative in the Qur'an as compared to the biblical original, send a clear message. In Sura 20, which is dedicated to the life of Moses, the handing over of the Torah, the stone tablets, is missing. There is only a passing

---

101 Neuwirth 2019, p. 405.

reference to it in a different chapter[102], despite this being the founding event of Judaism. Its marginalization actually amounts to the elimination of a central aspect of the Jewish history of election. Subsequently, the "Children of Israel" receive a grim warning: "Do not transgress ... lest My anger should descend upon you. And he upon whom My anger descends has certainly fallen." (Sura 20:81).

The historical reasons for this condemnation of the "Children of Israel" are simple. The Jews could not be convinced to support the war against Muhammad's hometown of Mecca, a project that was very close to his heart during his Medinan period.

The central event of the Qur'anic Musa narrative is his attempt to persuade the Pharaoh to let his people leave Egypt. In keeping with the biblical narrative, this attempt fails and the unbelieving Pharaoh is punished both in this world and in the hereafter, despite his "conversion" shortly before drowning in the Red Sea. From this narrative, which belongs to the literary genre of the 'punishment myth,' often used in the Qur'an, the devout reader of the Qur'an understands that Pharaoh is a cautionary example for all those who defy Muhammad's message.

In the biblical original, the Israelites clearly signal their willingness to accept the Torah of God that Moses brings to them. Two versions of this answer are reported in the Bible, "All that the LORD has said, we will hear and do." (Ex 24:7) and "we will listen and obey" (Dt 5:27). In the Qur'an, on the other hand, the Israelites' response to the gift of the Torah is turned into the exact opposite, with Sura 2:93 giving this biblical reference a vicious twist: here the Israelites say to God's offer, "We hear and disobey." This rejection of the Torah put into

---

[102] Sura 7:145: "And We [= Allāh] wrote for him [= Moses] on the tablets [something] of all things–instruction and explanation for all things."

the mouth of the Jews is extended in sura 4:46 to what was to become a 'classic' accusation against the Jews: "Among the Jews are those who distort words from their [proper] usages [...], twisting their tongues and defaming the religion. And if they had said [instead], 'We hear and obey' [...], it would have been better for them and more suitable. But Allāh has cursed them for their disbelief." This Qur'anic account of the Israelites' alleged response to the Torah is thus a blatant misrepresentation that claims to be biblical while actually negating the biblical wording. Thus the central event of Israel, the Mosaic covenant and the gift of the Torah, is turned into a central charge against the Jews.

The appropriation and merging of biblical figures in the Qur'an must be seen is the context of the evolution of Muhammad's relationship with the Jews, the phases of which are clearly discernible in the Islamic sacred text.

2.3 Phases in the relationships with the Jews

There are three distinct phases in the relationship between Muhammad and the emerging Islamic community. The spectrum of attitudes and actions ranges from consent to annihilation.

Phase 1 lasts from the first visions in Mecca in the year 610 to the hegira in the year 622. Here, Jews and Christians are grouped together under the name "People of the Book" or "People of the Scripture." Initially, Muhammad thinks that everything he proclaims in his prophetic ministry is of a piece with the teachings of "his predecessors," particularly with Moses and Jesus. Suras 30:2–5 even document his sympathy for Byzantium in view of its defeat at the hands of the Persian Sassanid. Suras 28:52–53 show that some Christians and Jews obviously recognized similarities between the proclamation of Muhammad and the biblical message and consequently gave him their approval. The Qur'an then turns these persons into

Muslims: "Those to whom We [= *Allāh*] gave the Scripture before it [= *the Qur'an*]–they are believers in it. And when it is recited to them, they say, 'We have believed in it; indeed, it is the truth from our Lord. Indeed we were, [even] before it, Muslims [submitting to Allāh]'."

By the end of this first phase, however, Muhammad starts to label some of the People of Scripture as unbelievers.[103]

Phase 2 begins with the hegira in 622. In Medina, a prosperous trading city, Muhammad encounters numerous learned Jews, some of whom even regarded him as a Jewish prophet. It was during this time that Jerusalem was to be faced during Muslim prayer. But barely two years later, Mecca was substituted for Jerusalem, which is the *Qiblah* until today.

In this phase Muhammad displays a conciliatory attitude to certain Jewish traditions while at the same time claiming them for himself. A vivid example of this is the so-called "night journey" undertaken by the Prophet in a kind of vision (as reflected also in the title of Sura 17 which describes this experience) during which he was transported "from al-Masjid al-Haram to al-Masjid al-Aqsa" (Sura 17:1). In the Tarif Khalidi translation, this reads: "from the Sacred Mosque [= *Mecca*] to the Furthest Mosque." The latter is generally taken to refer to the holy site in Jerusalem where Muhammad led other prophets in prayer and from where it is claimed he ascended to heaven. It is also close to the site of the destroyed Second Temple, the holiest site in Judaism. The assertion in Sura 17:1 is thus primarily a religious and political statement with far-reaching implications: Mecca is the center–everything else is periphery. It lays the foundation for the conflict-laden Islamic claim to this place up to this day.

---

103 For example, in Sura 3:100.

This vision reflects the theological idea of incorporating the Jewish biblical tradition into the Islamic belief system and its exploitation by that system for its own ends. The motivation for the visionary journey to Jerusalem is the biblical theme of the pilgrimage to Zion.[104] However, this is not about taking "instruction from Zion" (cf. Isa. 2:2 f.) as in the biblical model, but about declaring oneself Israel's heir. The adoption of Jewish customs, above all the dietary laws (sura 5:3–5), also dates from this time, with Muhammad in the same period also allowing (!) the Jews to eat everything that Muslims eat. Muhammad thus usurps the Jews' own traditions and declares himself the heir who is entitled to pass judgment on the disinherited.

This second phase also includes the Battle of Badr[105] in 624, in which Muhammad won an unexpected victory against the Meccans during one of his numerous caravan raids, which boosted his resolve to conquer his home town of Mecca. As local Jewish tribes could not be persuaded to support this war, "Muhammad rid himself of the Jews in several stages. Two tribes were exiled from the city *[= Medina]* and the third was the victim of a massacre."[106]

These expulsions, subjugations and extermination campaigns are closely associated with the name of the Khaybar oasis where

---

104 Cf. Psalm 122:1 f.: "I rejoiced when they said to me, 'Let us go to the house of the Lord.' And now our feet are standing within your gates, Jerusalem."

105 "According to the testimony of early Islamic tradition, Muhammad and about 300 of his followers had gone to Badr to intercept a rich Meccan caravan... [In the course of that] the Muslims suddenly came across a numerically superior Meccan army at Badr, which had moved out to protect the caravan and [the Muslims] inflicted on it a devastating defeat." (Maier 2001, p. 21).

106 Busse 1998, p. 20.

in 628 CE a battle was fought between its Jewish inhabitants and the Muslims, who emerged victorious. A complex conflict followed which, after a brief period of coexistence, finally ended with the expulsion of the Jews in 642 by Caliph Omar. He claimed that before his death Muhammad had commanded that two religions could not exist simultaneously in the Hejaz, i.e. the Arabian heartland.

This emblematic name *Khaybar* attracted attention again in 2017, when, following the recognition by the United States of Jerusalem as the capital of Israel, angry chants were heard in several European cities:

"Khaybar, Khaybar, ya yahud, Djaish Muhammad saya'ud."
"Khaybar, Khaybar, oh you Jews!
Muhammed's army will return."

It is therefore an open threat of expulsion and killing of Jews. In Israel, where the name "Khaybar" is well known as a type of Hezbollah rocket known as the Khaybar-1, there was shock and indignation that this call for destruction once again resounded in Europe and particularly in Germany without eliciting condemnation.

In **Phase 3**, as the Sharia or Islamic law was developed, the relationship with the Jews was characterized by a tolerance—bound to certain conditions. This came about by changed political-military circumstances arising from Muhammad's successful conquests.

How did this "moderation" come about? As the Muslim fighting community's sphere of power expanded, it became apparent that doing business with (living) Jews or Christians was more profitable than owning a depopulated oasis. At the same time, Muhammad had realized that he could not simply force Jews to embrace Islam, but freedom of worship was tied to certain contractual obligations. This development "paved the way for future policies toward all peoples with revealed Scriptures, regardless of denomination. It assured religious freedom and at the same time obliged them to pay a tax to the Muslims, usually in the form of a poll tax (gizya) (9:29)."[107] Jews and Christians under Muslim rule thus became "protected subjects" (dhimmis), one could also say second-class citizens–a defined status in Muslim countries to this day.

Access to the property of non-Muslims, as well as the introduction of the poll tax, which must be paid personally as a sign of humiliation,[108] may appear to be a form of tolerance. In reality, however, it represents the latent state of war that prevails between the "House of Islam" and the "House of War" pertaining to non-Muslims.

This is a situation of permanent war, which can easily be observed in many Muslim countries even today, particularly in relation to the death penalty which is legitimized and openly practiced in the event of apostasy from Islam. This practice is even justified by Ahmed al-Tayyeb, the current Grand Imam of Al-Azhar and former president of Cairo's Al-Azhar University, regarded in the West as a moderate and a sought-after interlocutor.[109]

---

107 Busse 1998, p. 49.
108 Cf. Nagel 2018, p. 565: "By handing over a head tax, a kind of penitential tax to atone for the refusal to enter Islam, combined with a gesture of humility, they [= the Dhimmis] can at least secure their lives."
109 In an interview of 16 June 2016, Ahmed al-Tayyeb delivered a precise answer to the question of what should happen to someone who leaves Islam: "The four schools of law agree that apostasy is a crime and that an apostate should be asked to repent, and if he does not, he should be killed". *https://www.mena-watch.com/mena-analysen-beitraege/der-papst-der-grossscheich-und-die-toleranz/* (accessed on 01/07/2019). Al-Tayyeb justifies the killing of

This third phase in the relationship with the Jews, does not imply any kind of agreement with Judaism as such or with individual Jews. Such phases of coexistence are in stark contrast to the sometimes-harsh pronouncements in the Hadith, the collections of Muhammad's sayings, which took shape in the centuries after his death. In one of these Hadiths, taught in schools and included in the Hamas Charter, the coming of the Last Judgement is linked to the annihilation of the Jews: "The Last Judgement will not come until the Muslims fight and kill the Jews; until the Jew hides behind the stones and trees, and the stone and the tree will say: O, you Muslim, o, you servant of Allāh, this is a Jew hiding behind me, come and kill him!"[110]

2.4 Questions concerning Qur'anic Anti-Judaism

Inner-Islamic approaches

There are some liberal Muslims who try to distance themselves from anti-Jewish statements in the Qur'an. One way of doing this is through the principle of "abrogation" ("naskh"), whereby Qur'an verses of an earlier date are cancelled or superseded by later ones if they contradict each other. There are also some Muslims who regard the Qur'an as a time-bound document set within a specific historical context which is therefore not authoritative for questions that go beyond personal piety. Moreover, there are attempts to declare the "mercy of God"

---

the apostate by referring to the danger it poses for Islamic society, comparable to high treason.

110 From the collection of Hadiths of Sahih al-Bukhari Book 4:6985:*https://web.archive.org/web/20171005173210/http://cmje.usc.edu/religious-texts/hadith/muslim/041-smt.php#041.6985* (accessed on 26/10/2019).

a Qur'anic leitmotif which would mean that all the individual statements of the Qur'an would have to be measured against that yardstick and, if necessary, rejected–including all statements relating to Anti-Judaism.

However, such approaches are at odds with certain Islamic principles such as Allāh's authorship of the Qur'an as well as the fundamental mission of subjecting the whole world to the "ongoing creative action of Allāh."[111] It is therefore doubtful whether such relativistic interpretations have a realistic chance of general acceptance among Muslims, for they must always face the weight of the authority of the Qur'anic text itself.

It is important, therefore, not to be under any illusions about the extent of Qur'anic-based hatred of the Jews within the Islamic community. It is a logical consequence of the Qur'anic assertions in this regard and is deeply rooted in Islamic tradition. This bitter insight is only slightly tempered by the long periods in history when the Jews have been much better off under Muslim rule than under that of their Christian counterparts.

An example of a Jewish voice on the Qur'an

The anti-Jewish polemics in the Qur'an could not fail to have a strong impact on those who experienced the scourge of Nazism. This was the case with the German commentator, writer and journalist, Ralph Giordano (1923–2014). After his traumatic experiences under the Nazi persecution of the Jews, he became a prominent figure in left-wing journalism in post-war West Germany. At the suggestion of his friend Chaim Noll, a

---

111 Cf., for example, Sura 2:255: "Allāh–there is no deity except Him, the Ever-Living, the Sustainer of [all] existence. Neither drowsiness overtakes Him nor sleep. To Him belongs whatever is in the heavens and whatever is on the earth."

perceptive German-Israeli writer, Giordano undertook to read the Qur'an in its entirety. In one of his publications, Noll quotes from a letter in which Giordano describes how this reading changed him: "I took it upon myself to read the Qur'an. From the first to the last, to the 114th Surah. It is a reading of terror and madness. It calls constantly for the killing of unbelievers, but above all of the Jews, the Jews, the Jews [...]. I can tell you this, after reading the Qur'an: the Qur'an is the most anti-Jewish book I have ever seen in my long life."[112]

A commission from a Christian perspective

Reaction to the recognition of the vicious nature of the Anti-Judaism in the Qur'an must not simply be confined to horror and outrage. Especially from a Christian perspective, these insights must lead to a commission. The Second Vatican Council has already stated that "God holds the Jews most dear for the sake of their Fathers; He does not repent of the gifts He makes or of the calls He issues."[113] However, this realization has only recently begun to enter general Christian consciousness. Even among Christians themselves, the assertion in the Gospel of John by Jesus has been neglected that "Salvation comes from the Jews" (John 4:22b). Pervasive anti-Jewish attitudes have become part of the history of Christianity and have all too often obscured the value of the Jewish story of salvation recounted in the Old Testament, to which this verse bears witness.

---

112 In a text by Chaim Noll on *www.achgut.com* from 28 June 2018 (accessed on 16/12/2018).
113 Declaration on the Relation of the Church to Non-Christian Religions *Nostra* aetate, No 4: http://www.vatican.va/archive/ hist_ councils/ii_vatican_council/documents/vat-ii_decl_19651028_ nostra-aetate_en.html (accessed on 03/04/2022).

The discovery of a sense of gratitude for this Jewish "history of salvation," which could benefit Christians and Muslims alike, would be the key to a greater appreciation of one's own traditions and to establishing a positive relationship with the Jews today.

Unlike the Qur'anic Ibrahim, Paul (cf. Gal 2:6–10) *extended* the Abrahamic lineage of the Jews to Christians –but did not supplant it. He never left the soil of Judaism, but worked passionately towards achieving the fulfilment of the promise of Abraham's blessing for all peoples. In Romans 11 he describes how the fruitful olive tree always remains Israel itself, onto which the Gentiles have been grafted. For Christians, therefore, being the "People of God" can only be conceived of *in conjunction with* Israel. This is the definitive Catholic position since the publication of *Nostra aetate*[114] by the Second Vatican Council.

Pope John Paul II gave the Catholic Church an important interpretative criterion. In a speech in the German city of Mainz in 1980 he said that the conversation with Israel is first and foremost a dialogue "within our Church, as it were between the first and second part of her Bible."[115] Israel's heritage is therefore not something external to the Church, which is why the Church is constantly committed to preserving this heritage for its own

---

114 Cf. *Nostra aetate* No. 4: "The Church, therefore, cannot forget that she received the revelation of the Old Testament through the people with whom God in His inexpressible mercy concluded the Ancient Covenant. Nor can she forget that she draws sustenance from the root of that well-cultivated olive tree onto which have been grafted the wild shoots, the Gentiles."

115 Taken from his speech to the representatives of the Cathedral museum in Mainz/Germany on 17 November 1980, cf. the Spanish translation, accessible at: *http://w2.vatican.va/content/john-paul-ii/es/speeches/1980/november/documents/hf_jp_ii_spe_19801117_ebrei-magonza.html* (accessed on 27/11/2019). There is no English translation available on the Vatican homepage. The

sake and by virtue of its own identity. It means that Jewish voices must *always* be included.

It follows that there can be no dialogue between Muslims and Christians that ignores or trivializes Qur'anic and Muslim Anti-Judaism. The acknowledgment of the catastrophic impact of Christian replacement theology on the Jews, and the effort on the part of Christians to correct this fundamental error, must also include a clear view on the pernicious stance taken in the Qur'an to obliterate Jewish salvation history and subsequently, the pervasive Muslim contempt of the Jewish people. Today's Christian response must be to work tirelessly to correct these past costly errors and to counter the misconceptions that fuel the anti-Jewish polemic.

The consequences of this insight range from the realm of "grand politics"–an example of which is the European adherence to the Nuclear Treaty with Iran, a nation that loses no opportunity to call for the annihilation of the State of Israel– to Muslim-Christian dialogue fora and everyday contacts with Muslims. The "never again" as a commitment in perpetuity in memory of the Holocaust must become an "Only *with* Israel," especially in contacts with Muslims.

---

original German version is accessible at: https://www.dbk.de/filead min/redaktion/veroeffentlichungen/verlautbarungen/VE_025A.pdf (p. 104; accessed on 06/09/2019).

3. Jesus in the Qur'an

3.1 Sources of the Qur'anic image of Jesus

The recourse to apocryphal sources

Similar to the Qur'anic portrayal of Abraham and Moses, the numerous mentions of Jesus[116] in the Qur'an serve primarily to legitimize its claim of being God's definitive revelation. In many cases, the Qur'an draws on the so-called "apocrypha." These are writings with Christian origins with legendary character or heretical, often Gnostic, tendencies. Therefore, the Church had not included them in the New Testament canon. The account of the Annunciation and a detail from Jesus' childhood narratives illustrate how these source texts were transformed.[117]

---

116 There is a wealth of research on the image of Jesus in the Qur'an. Notable for its balanced treatment of the subject is the following work, which forms the basis of this chapter: Räisänen, Heikki: Das Koranische Jesusbild. Ein Beitrag zur Theologie des Korans [The Qur'anic Image of Jesus. A Contribution to the Theology of the Qur'an]. Finnische Gesellschaft für Missiologie und Ökumenik: Helsinki 1971. Räisänen points out the importance "of discovering and understanding the original intentions ... of the Qur'an" (p. 13). He also highlights the problematic side of a dialogical (Christian) reading of the Qur'an that purports to be an "interreligious spiritual retreat" (p. 14), that is to say, a source of inspiring spiritual enrichment, but that in fact obscures the actual intentions of the Qur'an.

117 In this process of transformation, as in the case of other biblical figures, it is likely that Muhammad and the authors of the Qur'an obtained their information primarily from oral traditions and not from the texts themselves.

The New Testament account of the Annunciation in the Gospel of Luke, where the angel announces to Mary that she will bear a son, ends in Luke as follows: "Mary said, 'Behold, I am the handmaid of the Lord. May it be done to me according to your word.' Then the angel departed from her" (Luke 1:38). The apocryphal proto-gospel of James,[118] the main source[119] of the Qur'anic representation of Mary, also ends this scene in the same way. In the Qur'an, however, the Annunciation scene ends after Mary's objection ('How can I have a boy...?') as follows: "He [= *the messenger of the Lord'*] said: 'Thus [it will be]; your Lord says, 'It is easy for Me, and We will make him a sign to the people and a mercy from Us. And it is a matter [already] decreed.' So she conceived him, and she withdrew with him to a remote place."

The crucial difference compared to the original is that in the Qur'an Mary does not express her assent ("may it be done to me;" in the succinct Latin version: "fiat"), and that the angelic messenger states that it is "a matter [already] decreed" from Allāh's point of view. This small textual difference reveals a significant distinction: Mary's free collaboration in the biblical or apocryphal narrative becomes the enforcement of "a matter [already] decreed" in the Qur'an. With this shift in emphasis

---

118 Cf. Infancy Gospel of James 11, in: http://www.earlychristianwriti ngs.com/text/infancyjames-roberts.html (accessed on 21/02/2022).

119 Cf. Neuwirth 2019, p. 297. An example of how the image of Mary in the Qur'an clearly deviates from the biblical account is the merging in the Qur'an of Miriam, Moses' sister, with Mary, the mother of Jesus, to form one person: in the Qur'an, the father of the New Testament Mary is Amram (Arabic: Imram) who, in the biblical account, is the father of Moses, Aaron and Miriam (cf. 1 Chronicles 5:29). "Perhaps this 'error' is based on a typological interpretation that Muhammad had access to" (Busse 1998, p. 116).

the Qur'an sets a ground rule for the relationship between God and man: the free consent of the human being to Allāh's plan is not necessary, since for Allāh this plan is "a matter [already] decreed."

Theological voluntarism in the apocryphal sources

For centuries, Christianity struggled to come to an understanding of the true nature of Jesus Christ and to develop a language that would adequately express the insight reached. This lengthy and complex process lasted until the time of Islam's emergence: the last Christological dogma of the unity of the two wills in Jesus was formulated in 680/681.[120] The apocryphal Christian writings reflect this laborious process and bear witness to its evolution. In retrospect, the attempts made by heretics and the authors of the apocrypha to document their insights facilitated the discernment that ultimately led to the formulation of the major Christological dogmas of the early Church.

The problem, the repercussions of which are felt to this day, is that Muhammad and the co-authors of the Qur'an drew their information about Christianity mostly from these apocryphal writings–or from even more distorted oral information about these writings. Consequently, in a period of history when the search for Christian identity was still an ongoing theological process that needed to be refined and purged of inappropriate expressions, some of the emerging insights became part of the inviolable 'sacred' text of the Qur'an.

To better understand this phenomenon, let us consider by way of analogy the process of fermentation, which can be likened to the process of the historical development of Christology which, over time, clarified the true identity of Christ. During the

---

120 Cf. section 3.5, "A deeper understanding of Jesus".

biochemical fermentation process, different components interact with each other and are changed as a result. The authors of the Qur'an, however, isolated certain components of the theological fermentation process (the topics of Christological reflection), removed them prematurely from that evolutionary process and sacralized them in the Qur'an. Thus it was that still incomplete and embryonic theological positions were "frozen" in time, as it were, and came to be regarded by Muslims to this day as genuine representations of some of the core concepts of Christianity.

This situation can be illustrated by considering how the theological theme of divine omnipotence is treated in some apocryphal sources and then in the Qur'an.

Divine omnipotence is a recurring theme, for example, in the apocryphal Infancy Gospel of Thomas. As depicted there, the behavior of the boy Jesus could almost be termed reckless: by this account, Jesus caused the death, by his "word of authority," of a boy of a similar age who had collided with him.[121] The reaction of witnesses to this disturbing episode is described as follows: "When they saw what he [= the boy Jesus] had done, they were extremely afraid and did not know what to do. And they talked about him, saying, 'Every word he speaks, good or evil, is an event and becomes a miracle.' When Joseph saw that Jesus had done this, however, he was outraged and took his ear and pulled it extremely hard. Then, the child [=Jesus] became

---

121 Infancy Gospel of Thomas 4:1–2: "Next, he was going through the village again and a running child bumped his shoulder. Becoming bitter, Jesus said to him, 'You will not complete your journey.' Immediately, he fell down and died." In: http://www.earlychristianwritings.com/text/infancythomas.html (accessed on 21/01/2022).

angry and said to him [=Joseph], 'It is enough for you to seek and not find [...] Do not trouble me.' "[122]

To the modern reader this account may seem absurd, but at the time it served a single and specific purpose: to portray a divine omnipotence unfettered by any conventional ethical norms (it is said of Jesus' words: "whether good or bad") and shaped solely by the will. In the history of theology this is called "voluntarism."[123]

This emphasis on "the will," which is not bound to any moral categories, is somewhat softened at the end of the apocryphal narrative by the fact that all those who were "punished" by the boy Jesus are healed again.[124] This notion of an unfettered and even irrational divine omnipotence, which this kind of literature depicted as characterizing Jesus from his earliest years, came to full bloom in the Qur'an and in Islam where the unconstrained omnipotence of Allāh becomes the determining leitmotif.[125] Looking back on this development, it becomes clear how important it was for the Church to distance herself from this kind of voluntarism by excluding such writings from the canon.

---

122 Infancy Gospel of Thomas 5:3–6, ibid.
123 Interestingly, Pope Benedict XVI deals with this problem in a very particular way in his Lecture at the University of Regensburg in 2006. Cf. section 4.3 The Regensburg Address of Pope Benedict XVI.
124 Infancy Gospel of Thomas 8:3–4: "And when the child completed his speech, those who were under his curse were immediately saved, but from then on, nobody dared to make him angry because they did not want to be cursed or crippled." Ibid.
125 Cf. the remarks of Pope Benedict XVI (in section 4.3) on the necessity of overcoming theological voluntarism.

3.2 Basic features of the Qur'anic perception of Jesus

Representations of Jesus

The Qur'an talks about Jesus–Issa in Arabic–above all in the context of three larger textual units, namely, Suras 3:33–57, 5:110–120 and 19:1–33. The account of his life in the Qur'an is fragmentary rather than a cohesive whole, as can be seen, for example, in Sura 3:33–57. In total, Jesus is mentioned in fourteen suras and is thus "the most frequently mentioned biblical person next to Abraham and Moses."[126] The episodes associated with Jesus in the Qur'an–apart from a brief mention of his miracles and the selection of the disciples–are the Annunciation, his persecution by the Jews and his Ascension into heaven.

A most revealing source for the Qur'anic image of Jesus is Sura 19:1–33. This Sura dates from the Meccan period, when Muhammad had a more or less positive attitude towards Christians. Here the story of Jesus is embedded in the story of his mother, which it why it bears the name "Maryam" (= Mary).

As in the case of Luke's Gospel, Sura 19 recounts the childhood stories of John the Baptist and of Jesus in a parallel way. However, any Christological interpretation as found in the New Testament stories is consistently eliminated. In the Qur'an the person of John the Baptist has no function whatsoever for the development of Jesus' mission; the stories stand side by side but remain unconnected to each other.

The "speech" that the newborn Jesus gives in defense of his mother illustrates most clearly the key points of the Qur'anic perception of Jesus.

---

126 Gnilka, Joachim: Bibel und Koran [Bible and Qur'an]. Herder: Freiburg 2004, p. 105.

The defense speech of the infant Jesus in Sura 19

This speech begins when Maryam returns to her village with the newborn child and is accused of adultery: "So she *[= Mary]* pointed to him *[i.e. the boy Jesus]*. They said: 'How can we speak to one who is in the cradle a child?'" (Sura 19:29). The boy Jesus himself is made to answer this question: "[Jesus] said: 'Indeed, I am the servant of Allāh. He has given me the Scripture and made me a prophet. And He has made me blessed wherever I am and has enjoined upon me prayer and zakāh *[= a form of obligatory charity]* as long as I remain alive *[,]* And [made me] dutiful to my mother, and He has not made me a wretched tyrant. And peace is on me the day I was born and the day I will die, and the day I am raised alive.'" (Sura 19:30–33).

The first thing that stands out in this speech is how much Jesus, speaking about himself, has been conformed to the image of Muhammad: he is a "servant of Allāh," makes no claim to divinity, but has a divinely bestowed gift of blessing. Moreover, the attentive reader will see that this Isa behaves in accordance with the precepts of Islam–he prays, gives alms and declares his belief in the resurrection.

Another characteristic of this Qur'anic Jesus is that "the Scripture" (by which is meant the Gospel) was bestowed upon him. This term is repeatedly associated with Jesus in the Qur'an and is intended to establish an analogy: Moses was given the Torah, Jesus "the Gospel"–and Muhammad the Qur'an.

The fact that "Scripture" is referred to in the singular "corresponds to the specific Qur'anic conception not of four gospels *about* Jesus but rather of a revelation given to him."[127] What the Qur'an says about Muhammad was thus also in this

---

127 Neuwirth 2019, p. 299.

respect transferred to Jesus: *The Scripture* is not a report *about* Jesus but is rather something *given* to him.

Jesus as a prefiguration of Muhammad and a prophetic model

The authors of the Qur'an were aware of the theological disputes surrounding the person of Jesus. That is the backdrop against which Jesus is portrayed in the Qur'an as a "prophet" cast in a specific mold.

Sura 19 pursues this portrayal after the newborn child's defense speech: "That is Jesus, the son of Mary–the word of truth about which they are in dispute. It is not [befitting] for Allāh to take a son; exalted is He! *[i.e. far removed is he from any such need.]* When He decrees an affair, He only says to it, 'Be,' and it is. [Jesus said], 'And indeed, Allāh is my Lord and your Lord, so worship Him. That is a straight path.' Then the factions differed [concerning Jesus] from among them, so woe to those who disbelieved" (Sura 19:34–37).

This representation of Jesus in the Qur'an makes him the key witness for the preservation of "pure" monotheism, because of his categorical rejection of the title of the Son of God for himself. As such a proclaimer of a unified faith, he himself also calls for unity in faith. Jesus is thus portrayed as a "theologically disputed figure with the following firm motto …, that is frequently repeated in later suras:"[128] "Allāh is my Lord and your Lord, so worship Him. That is a straight path." (Sura 19:36). The disunity portrayed in verse 37 ("then the factions differed … from among them") alludes to the disputes concerning Jesus between Christians and Jews and among Christians themselves.

---

128 Neuwirth 2019, p. 300.

What the Qur'an says here about Jesus primarily reflects the situation of Muhammad and his emerging Islamic community, where fierce arguments were raging around their struggle for a "pure" monotheism. By this portrayal of Jesus as a prefiguration of Muhammad, the emerging Islamic community claimed him for their cause as another "prominent" authority.

Underlying this conception of Jesus is the schematization of a type of prophet that is found repeatedly in the Qur'an. This can be summarized as follows: The prophet proclaims the message of monotheism, and, in doing so, "is endowed by Allah with miracles of authentication to confirm his authority; he finds supporters and helpers, but even more adversaries who threaten his life. In the end he is saved by God's intervention."[129] This is the basic scheme of the prophetic model. The Qur'an molds the historical Jesus on this template, so that he, too, leads to Muhammad.

The rejection of the crucifixion of Jesus

A central characteristic of the Qur'anic image of Jesus is the denial of the crucifixion of Jesus in the form of a brief reference to it as a sham. This is only mentioned once in the Qur'an in Sura 4:157–158 in the context of an anti-Jewish diatribe: "And [for] their *[= the Jews']* saying, 'Indeed, we have killed the Messiah, Jesus, the son of Mary, the messenger of Allāh.' And they did not kill him, nor did they crucify him; but [another] was made to resemble him to them. And indeed, those who differ over it are in doubt about it. They have no knowledge of it except the following of assumption. And they did not kill him, for certain. Rather, Allāh raised him to Himself. And ever is Allāh Exalted in Might and Wise."

---

129 Busse 1998, p. 120.

This account is directed against both Jews and Christians. The two verses are framed by a long list of "wrongdoings" of the Jews (Sura 4:153–160). The Jews "were not accused of having killed Jesus, but of claiming to have done so."[130] But every Muslim takes from these verses of the Qur'an the message that the Jews are guilty in two ways: First, because they persecuted the "prophet Jesus" to the point of shedding his blood. And second, because they lie by concealing the reality–according to the logic of the Qur'an–of Jesus' salvation from crucifixion. According to this logic, the tragedy of Christians consists in the fact that they have believed this "lie" of the Jews, on which they, so says Muslim teaching, build their faith to this day. Consequently, every cross that a Muslim sees has the effect of reawakening these suspicions and distortions.

The recourse to Docetism

By teaching Jesus' salvation from the "danger of crucifixion" the Qur'an is inspired by the doctrine of "Docetism." This is a concept derived from the Greek word "dokein," which has the meanings of "seeming" and "appearing." Docetism refers to an early Christian heresy which ascribes to Jesus not a real but only an *apparent* human existence and therefore only *apparent* suffering. In reality, according to this heretical concept, Jesus, as "true God", remained untouched by all this. This denial of the full humanity of Jesus is molded by Greek philosophical ideas which put inner or spiritual "knowledge" ("gnosis") above the real "redemption" of human life *in its totality*. The Docetism that is evident in the Qur'an was the fruit of a Gnostic-heretical environment with its sharply drawn distinction between matter

---

130 Busse 1998, p. 132.

and spirit. This Gnostic environment in turn shaped the Qur'anic authors' conception of the prophetic office.

This Jesus-Isa, and the end of his earthly life in accordance with the schematization of a rescued prophet, is of course a falsification of history. Apart from the consistent reports about the crucifixion in the Gospels, it is in fact the *scandal* of a crucified Messiah that speaks most eloquently for the authenticity of what happened. From the point of view of his followers, a much more obvious reaction would have been not to accord this "scandalous" fate of their Messiah such a central place, but to ignore it. The Qur'an's rejection of this historical event thus reflects precisely the attitude that the crucifixion of a righteous man was a barely acceptable scandal.

However, the Qur'anic narrative is based on the fundamental theological misunderstanding that man is not a free participant in the divine plan of salvation. This misunderstanding also applied to the Qur'anic Jesus as a human being.

The Qur'an leaves open the further fate of Jesus, i.e. whether he died a natural death or whether he was permanently "saved." The view of Jesus' death and salvation presented here is in any case decisive for the Islamic image of Jesus. So, for example, Muhammad ibn Jarir al-Tabari (839–923), an authoritative Muslim commentator on the Qur'an, interprets the crucifixion of Jesus as merely an apparent death (in keeping with the view of Docetism), followed by his subsequent salvation. In so doing, al-Tabari reproduces some of the stories circulating at the time, all deceptive, which also incorporated Gnostic and possibly even Manichaean tendencies.[131]

---

131 Cf. also Simon 1997, p. 139: "The apparent crucifixion of Jesus is ultimately a doctrine that Muhammad probably heard in a Gnostic-Manichaean context." Cf. section 1.3 Manichaean Elements.

Jesus as the eschatological accuser of the Christians

After the denial of the crucifixion, Sura 4:159 goes one step further, declaring that Jesus-Isa will be a witness at the Last Judgment ("on the day of resurrection") with regard to the "people of the Scripture." Christ as the judge of the world in the Christian context has thus become, in the Qur'anic version, an accusatory witness against the Christians, with Allāh as arbiter. Jesus is thus on a par with many other "witnesses" who will have to appear before Allāh with their community at the Final Judgment. For example, Sura 10:47 reads: "And for every nation is a messenger. So when their messenger comes *[to witness on the Day of Judgment]*, it will be judged between them in justice, and they will not be wronged."

At this final judgment there will also be a verdict on the Christian image of God. However, the Qur'an presents a distorted picture of the purported Christian image of God, portraying the Christian Trinity as consisting of God, Jesus and Mary. Sura 5:116 clothes this idea as a reproach of Allāh to Jesus: "O Jesus, Son of Mary, did you say to the people, 'Take me and my mother as deities besides Allāh?'" Of course, Jesus rejects this absurd accusation.

There has been much speculation as to the source of this peculiar conception of the Trinity. It is possible that the authors of the Qur'an may have been influenced by interactions with heretical Christians, such as the "Philomarianites."[132] Besides

---

[132] This Christian sect, also known as the "Collyridians", interpreted the Theotokos title of Mary (Mary as the "Bearer of God") in the sense of the elevation of Mary to a quasi-divine status and her appointment as "Priestess of the New Covenant". Räisänen refers to the fact that "in Syria in particular ... it has been customary from time immemorial to assemble a divine father, a divine mother and a divine son into a family of gods." (Räisänen 1971, p. 84).

rejecting this conception of the Trinity, the Qur'anic Jesus is also reproachful of the fact that it was developed contrary to his own intentions (Sura 5:117b) after the Ascension (in the words of this verse: when Allāh "took him up"). So the function of the Qur'anic Jesus here is to criticize the Christians "who do not understand." Allāh is portrayed as willing to tolerate the false doctrines of men in the period between the Ascension of Jesus and the Day of Judgment when finally he will chastise them (Sura 5:118–120).

The Qur'anic image of Jesus has an effect–albeit indirectly–on the daily prayer life of every devout Muslim. For the frequently uttered short prayer "Basmala" ("In the name of Allāh, the Most Gracious, the Most Merciful"), the central invocation at the beginning of every Quranic sura and in Islamic prayer practice up to this day, may have had its origin in a deliberately revised formulation of the trinitarian introductory prayer: "In the name of the Father and of the Son and of the Holy Spirit."

3.3 Qur'anic argumentation against the divinity of Jesus

Argumentation patterns

As we have seen, the rejection of the divinity of Jesus relies on various arguments, which the authors of the Qur'an derived mainly from the Jewish or Christian-heretical environment. The fact, for example, that Jesus did eat food leads to the conclusion that he was a man and not God.[133] The authors of the Qur'an say that the "creation" of Jesus in the body of Mary is an analogous

---

133 Cf. Sura 5:75: "The Messiah, son of Mary, was not but a messenger; [other] messengers have passed on before him ... They both [= *Jesus and his mother*] used to eat food." This is

process to the creation of Adam from dust.[134] When Christians attempt to refute such arguments by means of scriptural evidence, they are accused of being falsifiers of scripture.[135]

Apart from fundamental theological misunderstandings, these arguments again reveal that the Qur'an does not reflect authentic Christian beliefs but rather, that it echoes the voices heard in the mostly polemical theological debates that were raging at the time. The fact that these voices have been preserved in the Qur'an is interesting from a historical perspective, for the Qur'an thus proves to be a repository of heresies and theological misunderstandings. From an enlightened theological perspective, for example, the fact that Jesus did eat cannot be an argument against his divinity since the "divine nature" of Jesus does not stand in opposition to normal human processes in the life of Jesus. The human nature of Jesus, with all that it entails, is–as is expressed by the Council of Chalcedon in 451–"unconfused" with his divine nature. The correct understanding of this theological statement is therefore highly relevant.

The title "Son of God"

The decisive point of controversy in relation to Christology concerns the title "Son of God."[136] What the Qur'an here rejects

---

followed by the accusation that, despite this evidence, Christians nevertheless deify Jesus.

134 Cf. Sura 3:59: "Indeed, the example of Jesus to Allāh *[i.e. regarding His creation of him]* is like that of Adam. He created him from dust; then He said to him, 'Be,' and he was."

135 Cf. Sura 3:78: "And indeed, there is among them a party *[= Christians]* who alter the Scripture with their tongues so you *[= Muslims]* may think it *[i.e. what they say]* is from the Scripture, but it is not from the Scripture."

136 It is a matter of debate in Qur'anic research whether the criticism expressed in the Qur'an is directed against Christian ideas of the

is not the actual Christian standpoint on the issue, but rather concerns what the Qur'an's authors understood it to be. Thus in Sura 19:88 the "disbelievers" are quoted as saying, "The Most Merciful has taken [for Himself] a son"–which is then sharply rejected. The Arabic word used here for a (male) child is *walad*, meaning a physically begotten descendant. Here and elsewhere in the Qur'an, the main motive for the criticism of the title "Son of God" is the desire to preserve the absolute sovereignty of God.[137]

The Niceno-Constantinopolitan Creed affirmed that Christ, as *the eternal Son* ("born of the Father before all ages"), is "begotten, *not* made".[138] The focus of this formulation is not "begotten," but rather the *rejection* of the notion of Jesus being a creature, i.e. "not made." This was intended to avert a *theological* misunderstanding: Jesus Christ is not a creature

---

Trinity and the Son of God, or rather, against *pagan* "God-son/God-daughter" traditions. Sura 53:21 at any rate asks critically whether certain female figures popular with the Meccans were rightfully "to be addressed as daughters of God", and Sura 43:58 shows that the Meccans perceived Jesus as a competitor to their own deities. It is therefore conceivable that the authors of the Qur'an had an anti-pagan rather than an anti-Christian polemic in mind.

137 Thus even the merely figurative use of the title "Son of God," as in the Bible, is emphatically rejected, as for instance in Sura 5:18: "But the Jews and the Christians say, 'We are the children of Allāh and His beloved.' Say, 'Then why does He punish you for your sins?' Rather, you are human beings from among those He has created. He forgives whom He wills, and He punishes whom He wills. And to Allāh belongs the dominion of the heavens and the earth and whatever is between them, and to Him is the [final] destination."

138 Originally, the Creed was written in Greek, but in the well-known Latin version the wording is "genitum, non factum."

among other creatures; he is not simply a part of creation, albeit a particularly important one, as Arianism had been teaching for centuries. In its use of the wording "begotten, not made", on the other hand, the Creed is based on the New Testament account in Lk 1:35, according to which Jesus was "spiritually begotten", thus continuing the tradition already evident in the Old Testament where, in Psalm 2:7, God says to "his anointed one": "You are My son; today I have begotten you."

These theological insights were not accessible to Muhammad who only took up *the distorted image* of the Sonship of God, in which God was physically involved in procreation.

3.4 Jesus in current Muslim-Christian thinking

The approach of Comparative Theology

Towards the end of the 20th century in the USA–in response to the growing global religious and cultural diversity–the so-called "Comparative Theology" movement emerged, especially among Catholic theologians. Its objective was to learn from other religious traditions, but at the same time to remain rooted in one's own religious tradition. The initiator of this theological direction, the American Jesuit and religious scholar Francis Clooney, defines this approach as follows: "This learning is sought for the sake of fresh theological insights that are indebted to the newly encountered tradition(s) as well as the home tradition."[139] This marked a shift of emphasis in relation to the preceding so-called "theology of religious pluralism," which had

---

139 Clooney, Francis X.: Comparative Theology: Deep Learning Across Religious Borders. Wiley-Blackwell: Chichester 2010, p. 10.

tried to explain the differences between religions above all by attributing them to different religious "lenses."

Through a better knowledge of other religions, Comparative Theology seeks to lead Christianity itself to a higher degree of "truth." A necessary precondition, however, is the detachment from previous apologetics, which, in the comparison of religions–in this view–only want to demonstrate the superiority of their own religion.

It must be said, however, that such detachment from apologetics reveals a mistaken view of the main concern of the early Christian "apologists," which was to understand and define what constitutes what is specifically Christian and what is not. Through their efforts the "apologists" built upon the religion-critical process of discernment already present in the Old Testament, which corresponds to a certain view of the world and God's place in it.[140] Comparative Theology distances itself from this tradition of apologetic discernment because it limits Christianity to the exclusively religious sphere.[141]

The Comparative Approach and the Qur'anic question about Jesus

The Catholic theologian Klaus von Stosch, the authoritative representative of this theological approach[142] in the

---

140 Cf. for example, Psalm 115:1–9.
141 For example, Francis X. Clooney, in a biographical review of the genesis of comparative theology, reports how his teaching in a Hindu-Buddhist environment in Nepal changed him: "I had to learn in order to teach, and my Hindu and Buddhist students taught me much about how to think, act, and love religiously." (Clooney 2010, p. 18).
142 The dialogue between the proponents of Comparative Theology and Muslim scholars is strongly supported by the German State.

Jesus in current Muslim-Christian thinking 87

German-speaking world, starts from the premise that "through the encounter with other religions we learn decisive things about God and his revelation in Christ."[143] When this approach is applied to Christian-Muslim dialogue, its main aim is to seek to clarify the issue of Jesus.

What does this attempt look like concerning the Qur'anic image of Jesus?

Together with the Muslim theologian Mouhanad Khorchide, Von Stosch makes an attempt to reconcile the Christian and the Qur'anic approach to this issue by posing the question "whether it is conceivable from the Christian side to recognize the Qur'anic appraisal of Jesus of Nazareth as a Christology that also has something to say to Christians, [...] whether one can discover in the strangeness of this approach an enrichment of one's own identity."[144] In considering this question, the image of Jesus that is portrayed both in the Sunni and in the much broader Shiite Qur'anic tradition, is subjected to critical scrutiny. The question is repeatedly raised as to whether "mutual learning processes can occur without leveling out the differences between the two religions."[145]

On the basis of a historical-literary exegesis of the Qur'an, there is a detailed analysis of the evolution of the perception

---

Von Stosch and his Muslim interlocutor, Mouhanad Khorchide, have at their disposal a government-funded interreligious working group, the Deutsche Forschungsgemeinschaft (DFG) (German Research Foundation).

143 Von Stosch 2019, p. 355.
144 Von Stosch, Klaus, Khorchide, Mouhanad (Eds.): Streit um Jesus: Muslimische und christliche Annäherungen [Controversy over Jesus: Muslim and Christian approaches]. Schöningh: Paderborn 2016, p. 7.
145 Von Stosch 2016, p. 8.

of Jesus as the Qur'an itself evolved. So what emerges is an image of Jesus which, from a historical point of view, is quite differentiated. Von Stosch repeatedly emphasizes that he wants to preserve his own Christian identity, but he refuses to interpret it from an "exclusively" Christian point of view: "My principal interest is expressly not apologetic, and I want to avoid, if possible, proposing interpretations that contradict the Qur'an from the Muslim point of view [...]. The perspective chosen here thus aims to take the Qur'an seriously as a significant text, possibly divine in origin, and to respect Muslim traditions of interpretation of this text and to include them in my own interpretation as contemporary Muslim interpretations."[146]

Von Stosch comes to the conclusion that the Qur'an is undoubtedly ready "to confirm some of the central points of departure of Christology, but in the same breath warns against erroneous developments in Christian theology."[147] He identifies the absolute sovereignty of God's actions as the decisive criterion for the formation of the Qur'anic image of Jesus. Von Stosch summarizes the resulting new, "Qur'an-sensitive" Christian view of Jesus as follows: "Perhaps it is possible, after all [...] to affirm, with the Qur'an, that the distinctive feature that set Jesus apart is that he is so filled with the Spirit of God that he becomes for us the Word of God and illustrates to us by his life and his teachings what it means to be a servant of God and becomes, precisely by virtue of that fact, an exemplary person."[148]

This goes to the heart of the issue that must be considered here.

---

146 Von Stosch, Klaus: Versuch einer ersten diachronen Lektüre der Jesusverse im Koran [Attempt at a first diachronic reading of the Jesus verses in the Qur'an]. In: Von Stosch 2016, p. 16.
147 Von Stosch 2016, p. 43.
148 Von Stosch 2016, p. 43 f.

Questions on the Comparative Approach

The Qur'an repeatedly rejects Christian teachings that, within Christian context, have in fact proved to be heresies or misunderstandings. Thus many judgments in the Qur'an have little to do with authentic Christian faith. Apart from this useful insight brought forth by the Comparative Approach, some critical questions remain to be asked about this approach.[149]

The fundamental question is whether a reading of Jesus that is "Qur'an-sensitive" can identify different points of view without in reality submitting to certain Qur'anic pre-conceptions. As previously stated, Von Stosch "does not wish to be apologetic" or "to propose interpretations that contradict the Qur'an."[150] However, this can only mean that Christian beliefs have been adapted to accommodate the Qur'anic view.

The second, related, critical question is whether the "Christian" view represented here is not already so diluted and tailored to supposed "pastoral suggestions" that it no longer reflects the breadth of Christian theology. This is the impression one gets when Von Stosch repeatedly tries to translate details of the Qur'anic image of Jesus into pastoral suggestions for contemporary Christians. Thus, for example, he recommends that the defense speech of the newborn infant Jesus in Sura

---

149 That there is a correlation between this theology and certain political attitudes is shown by the fact that, in February 2018, Von Stosch was awarded the World Award for Book of the Year of the Islamic Republic of Iran by Hassan Rohani, the President of that country. In view of this State's repeatedly expressed desire to destroy the State of Israel and the brutal suppression of its domestic opposition, this is an extremely ambivalent honor. Surprisingly, however, even the Catholic media in Germany consistently reported positively on this "honor."

150 Von Stosch 2016, p. 16.

19:30–33 be seen as an intuitive insight that "invites us to look at the abilities and talents of babies and children with a new awareness."[151] The early Church, with its "apologists" maligned by this approach, displayed considerably more theological expertise when it rejected such legendary constructs.

However, even more serious than this kind of pastoral infantilization is the serious theological problem associated with this approach.

In order to recognize the extent of this problem one has to recall one of the fundamental documents of the Second Vatican Council which states: "At all times and in every race, God has given welcome to whosoever fears Him and does what is right (cf. Acts 10:35). God, however, does not make men holy and save them merely as individuals, without bond or link between one another. Rather has it pleased Him to bring men together as one people, a people which acknowledges Him in truth and serves Him in holiness. He therefore chose the race of Israel as a people unto Himself. With it He set up a covenant. Step by step He taught and prepared this people."[152]

This means that the actual subject of every theology is God himself who, since Abraham, has endeavored to gather a People in this world through whom he has desired to prepare the "salvation" of the whole world, using this people as his "instrument." Consequently, it is not primarily the individual believer who should give greater attention at a particular detail, even if the People of God is of course dependent on every single individual among them. To narrow theology down to an "enrichment" of

---

151 Von Stosch 2016, p. 19.
152 Dogmatic Constitution on the Church *Lumen Gentium*, Vatican Council II, 21 November 1964, No. 9. https://www.vatican.va/archive/hist_councils/ii_vatican_council/documents/vat-ii_const_19641121_lumen-gentium_en.html (accessed on 21/04/2020).

the individual life of faith would mean abandoning the foundation that this biblical heritage represents. Instead of seductively simple pastoral suggestions relating to a "Qur'an-sensitive" Jesus, what is needed is to recall anew that all theological discourse is rooted in the People of God to which the Bible bears witness, and which includes both Israel and the church.[153]

The examination of the Qur'anic image of Jesus could therefore be made fruitful in a completely different way. The apparent streamlining of biblical figures for one's own purposes, displayed in the Qur'an, should become the starting point for rediscovering the figure of Jesus on the basis of original sources: the biblical witnesses and the reflections of the Church in the first millennium. The following section constitutes a contribution to such a deeper understanding of Jesus.

3.5 A deeper understanding of Jesus

The challenge of cultural diversity

A new and more profound understanding of Jesus has for some time been confronted with the challenge of the "inculturation"

---

[153] A noteworthy comment in this regard is found, for example, in Pope Francis' Post-Synodal Apostolic Exhortation *Querida Amazonia* of February 2020, in which he emphasizes in No 33 the importance, especially for young people, of being aware of one's own roots: "For those of them who are baptized, these roots include the history of the people of Israel and the Church up to our own day. Knowledge of them can bring joy and, above all, a hope capable of inspiring noble and courageous actions." Source: https://www.vatican.va/content/francesco/en/apost_exhortations/documents/papa-francesco_esortazione-ap_20200202_querida-amazonia.html (accessed on 15/03/2020).

of Christianity in foreign cultures.[154] This question is of central importance, because often in the course of colonial history the impression was created of Jesus being a white European, as pictorial representations attest to this day. The reaction to this situation has been a "post-colonial theology" which often subjects traditional theological positions to undifferentiated and sweeping criticism.

What would be an appropriate approach today to achieving a deeper understanding of Jesus?

The tradition of Israel as corrective

The Protestant exegete, Julius Wellhausen (1844–1918), had, already at the beginning of the 20th century, come to the conclusion that Jesus was not a Christian but a Jew: "He did not proclaim a new faith, but taught how to do the will of God. For him, as for the Jews, the will of God was embodied in the law and in the other Holy Scriptures that were added to it."[155] Since then, this basic insight has been repeatedly reiterated. Thus the Declaration *Nostra aetate* of the Second Vatican Council (1965) states with reference to the New Testament Letter of St Paul to the Romans: "The Church keeps ever in mind the words of the Apostle about his kinsmen: 'theirs is the sonship and the

---

154 Cf. the document *Faith and Inculturation* (1988) of the Vatican's International Theological Commission: https://www.vatican.va/roman_curia/congregations/cfaith/cti_documents/rc_cti_1988_fede-inculturazione_en.html (accessed on 15/03/2020) which states: "Inculturation which borrows the way of dialogue between religions cannot in any way pledge itself to syncretism." (Ch. III: Present Problems of Inculturation, No. 14: The Transcendence of the Gospel in Relation to Culture).

155 Wellhausen, Julius: Einleitung in die Drei Ersten Evangelien [Introduction to the First Three Gospels]. Georg Reimer: Berlin

A deeper understanding of Jesus

glory and the covenants and the law and the worship and the promises; theirs are the fathers and from them is the Christ according to the flesh' (Rom. 9:4–5), the Son of the Virgin Mary. She also recalls that the Apostles, the Church' s main-stay and pillars, as well as most of the early disciples who proclaimed Christ's Gospel to the world, sprang from the Jewish people."[156]

Much has been written about this since then[157] in Church documents.[158] In catechesis and preaching, too, these connections became an important theme–or this should at any rate be the case according to authoritative Church statements. Cardinal Jean-Marie Lustiger highlighted the centrality of this question: "But the mystery of Israel remains at the center of the Christian faith. If we consider it unessential, we expose just how far we are from being Christian."[159] With regard to an adequate understanding of Jesus, Cardinal Lustiger drew the following conclusion: "Pagans, even when they become Christians, are constantly tempted to refuse the particularity of history and divine election. They are tempted to make Jesus the projection of the ideal man that each culture and civilization creates within itself. That is the most

---

1905, p. 113. There were Jewish authors who had come to similar insights even earlier, but had not found a receptive audience at the time.

156 *Nostrae aetate*, No. 4 (cf. footnote 114).
157 Cf., for example, the comprehensive explanations in: Hengel, Martin and Schwemer, Anna Maria: Jesus and Judaism. Mohr Siebeck: Tübingen 2019.
158 Cf., for example, Notes on the correct way to present Jews and Judaism in preaching and catechesis in the Roman Catholic Church, published in 1985 by the Vatican Commission for Religious Relations with the Jews.
159 Lustiger, Jean-Marie: The Promise. Wm. B. Eerdmans Publishing Co.: Grand Rapids, Michigan/Cambridge, U.K. 2007, p. 93.

instinctive way of bringing God down to man's scale–in other words, of falling into idolatry by worshiping oneself. Each pagan civilization that becomes Christian is likely to be enticed into making Jesus its Apollo and projecting on him its own image of man, an image that it finds pleasing."[160]

Even though Lustiger was describing a danger facing cultures that have become Christian, his observations can also be applied to the Qur'anic misunderstanding of Jesus: Jesus was conformed to the image of Muhammad, or rather a schematized ideal "prophet." The Qur'anic distortion of Jesus can thus be seen as a warning against the potential dangers posed by enculturation processes within Christianity. Other examples of this are the denial of the crucifixion in order to align the real fate of Jesus with that of the Qur'anic prophetic scheme (cf. Sura 4:157–158), and Jesus apparent knowledge of his own mission already from birth, as revealed in the speech of the infant Jesus (cf. Sura 19:30–33).

The Qur'anic perception of Jesus is in fact the prime example of a failed appropriation: It is not the real, biblically attested Jesus who becomes decisive for the culture that receives him, but rather, it is the culture that shapes an image of Jesus according to its own standards. In the Qur'an, the crucified Messiah of Israel has become the Jesus who, under the leadership of Muhammad, is to guide "his" unruly Christendom to submission to the rule of Allāh.

A historical analogy for such a distortion is Arianism, whose doctrine of Jesus' submission to God the Father kept the ancient Church in thrall for centuries. Initially, this false doctrine appealed in particular to the Frankish-Germanic tribes

---

160 Lustiger, Jean-Marie: Choosing God, Chosen by God. Ignatius Press: San Francisco 1991, p. 64.

A deeper understanding of Jesus   95

whose essential cultural orientation could conceive of only *one* military commander or only *one* tribal prince. Consequently, the idea of "equality" among the members of a Trinity was all but incomprehensible for this mentality. They were therefore already largely Arian by virtue of their cultural disposition and they then transferred their ideas of subordination to Jesus and his "position" within the Trinity.

At the same time, the Church's own Christology is also a decisive corrective to ward off distortions of the image of Jesus and to contribute to a deeper understanding of Jesus. This becomes apparent by highlighting an important Christological dogma that is often forgotten.

The rediscovered unification of divine and human free will in Jesus

The starting point for the discussion that follows is a historical coincidence. Exactly at the time of the Islamic conquests of the 7th century, the Third Council of Constantinople (680–681) clarified an issue that had been left open at the Council of Chalcedon (451): it affirmed that Jesus was *fully* human and that he had *freely* subordinated his will to that of God. Following the insights of the theologian Maximus Confessor (c. 580–662, and so in fact a contemporary of Muhammad!), the Third Council of Constantinople condemned the so-called "monotheletism": the heresy that Jesus had only one will, namely, the divine will. The supposition was that he had been a kind of divine being on earth, who only outwardly had a human form. According to this heresy, the human (free) will of Jesus would have had no other option than to submit to his divine nature.

But this one-sided view of Jesus is contradicted by what was stated about him in the Letter to the Hebrews: "In the days when he was in the flesh, he offered prayers and supplications with loud cries and tears to the one who was able to save him from death ... Son though he was, he learned obedience from what he suffered" (Heb 5:7–8). In a similar way, the Synoptic Gospels tell of the prayer of Jesus on the Mount of Olives, in which Jesus, faced with the threat of the Passion, turns to the Father: "Father, if You are willing, remove this cup from Me; yet not My will, but Yours be done." (Luke 22:42). Based on this, the Third Council of Constantinople affirms: "And we proclaim equally two natural volitions or wills in him and two natural principles of action which undergo no division, no change, no partition, no confusion."[161] On this basis, the Council rejects the notion "of only a single natural principle of action of both God and creature."[162]

Why is this theological insight important for a clearer understanding of Jesus in the face of the Qur'anic image of Jesus?

On the one hand, as in the Qur'an, this dogma affirms God's sublimity, his effectiveness, which cannot be diminished. On the other hand–in contrast to the Qur'an–the freedom of man is acknowledged. Jesus used his human freedom, i.e. his "will," to put himself at the disposal of the will of God and his work in the world. The epochal aspect of this discovery was described as follows by the Catholic theologian Ludwig Weimer, with reference to Maximus Confessor, to whom the Third Council of Constantinople owes this insight: "Maximus understood very clearly that ... the solution did not lie in making a non-human out of Jesus, but rather, in developing a correct concept of freedom which could be defined as follows: to be free is to willingly consent to the will of God."[163]

---

161 https://www.papalencyclicals.net/councils/ecum06.htm (accessed on 22/02/2022).
162 Ibid.
163 Weimer, Ludwig: Die Lust an Gott und seiner Sache [Taking delight in God and his cause]. Herder: Freiburg 1981, p. 117.

If one compares this insight with corresponding statements in the Qur'an, it becomes clear that Islam is stuck in a kind of monotheletism. There is only the all-dominant will of Allāh, accentuated by Muhammad's personal history and experience, to which man has to submit. Subsequently, it is secondary whether this submission takes place with or without the free consent of the human will.

This theological cornerstone of Islam has far-reaching consequences, as it makes religious freedom and even democracy on an Islamic basis impossible, as has become evident today. The centuries-long Christological struggle, on the other hand, has created the spiritual basis for an image of God, and also an image of man, that values human freedom and that, over a period of centuries, has enabled the development of the awareness of a universal human dignity.

The Christological dogma of 681 we have been speaking of here was a milestone on the way to this mature conception of God and man. On the political level, the separation from monotheletism paved the way for the farewell to theocracy. On the theological level, the dogma of dyotheletism (= two wills in Jesus) constituted a return to the biblical view of man: the second biblical account of creation already recognizes man's freedom to orientate himself towards the will of God or to oppose it, through the image of the "tree of the knowledge of good and evil" (Gen 2:17). In other words, the human being has a real choice.

The repositioning of the person of Jesus as an integral part of the tradition of Israel, together with the revitalization of ecclesiastical Christology, bears an enormous potential. That is, in response to God's affection to accept freely and gladly the divine will of salvation, *beyond submission*.

The concluding chapter discusses the reflections on Islam of two prominent authors, one Jewish, the other Christian. Due to the clarity of their analyses and their conclusions, they are more relevant for our times than ever.

4. Franz Rosenzweig and Joseph Ratzinger on Islam

4.1 Islam as an overall phenomenon

After the overview in the preceding three chapters of the sources and core content of the Qur'an, this fourth chapter poses certain crucial questions to Islam and attempts to arrive at some theological answers. An early 20th century Jewish philosopher, Franz Rosenzweig (1886–1929), and a Pope who held office at the beginning of the 21st century (2005–2013), Benedict XVI/Joseph Ratzinger (*1927), provide astonishing insights in this regard.

In their analyses, Islam is not described in the way that it would prefer itself to be seen. The perspectives that emerge have become unfamiliar over the years and are consequently considered by many to be harsh. It is therefore important to point out that these insights are neither a personal devaluation of certain believers nor do they present a general suspicion of all Muslims, nor a relapse into petty comparisons of religions in the sense, for example, of the fratricidal quarrel in Lessing's Ring Parable. In contrast to the Ring Parable,[164] the two authors featured here are not concerned with judging whether Jews, Christians or Muslims behave in a praiseworthy manner according to their respective ethos ("Who proves to be the true heir by his actions?"). Rosenzweig and Ratzinger are not concerned with *devaluation*, but rather, with *revaluation*–with restoring the value of redemption, of liberation and ultimately, of the salvation of this world.

---

164 This refers to the popular play by the German author, Gotthold Ephraim Lessing, *Nathan the Wise* (1799), a fervent plea for religious tolerance.

In what follows, Islam will be considered as a composite whole in an effort to distill its essence, as it were. Differentiations such as those drawn between Sunnis and Shiites, or the customary distinction made in the West between "Islamic" and "Islamist",[165] fall outside the scope of this discussion.

This chapter's shift from the Qur'an to Islam in general, calls for a short linguistic explanation of the word "Islam." In Arabic, the verb "aslama" from which the word "Islam" is derived, means "to give up, to submit, to surrender, to give into, or to hand over." Where, in certain expressions, this verb is also connected with the object "the face," it implies the handing over or surrendering of the whole person. "Islam," the noun form of this verb, in its literal sense thus means "submission," "surrender" or "giving up," and tellingly, it is also the name of the religion founded by Muhammad. The suggestion sometimes made that the word "Islam" is derived from the Arabic word as-salām, meaning "peace", is feasible in purely lexical terms. It would however obscure the real meaning of the word. In contrast to the meaning of the word "peace" in the Western sense, as-salām means "the dominion of Allāh established by the social and military measures of Muhammad and his successors."[166] Accordingly, the "House of Peace" is the part of the world which is subject to Muslim rule.

---

165 Interestingly enough, this distinction is rejected as absurd by well-known Islamic authors themselves, for example, by Dr Shabbir Akhtar, a member of the Faculty of Theology and Religions at the University of Oxford, who considers this distinction a Western invention that completely misses the reality of Islamic self-understanding (cf. Footnote 25 and: Akhtar 2011, p. 4).

166 Nagel 2018 (cf. Footnote 1), p. 47. Cf. also Sura 4:125: "Who is more excellent in religion than he who surrenders his face wholly to God [...]?" (Tarif Khalidi translation; cf. footnote 99).

In the light of the numerous questions that this worldview entails, Franz Rosenzweig and Joseph Ratzinger offer remarkable analyses of Islam as an overall phenomenon.

4.2 Franz Rosenzweig's view on Islam

Biographical context

As early as 1920, showing great foresight, the German-Jewish philosopher Franz Rosenzweig wrote in his lecture notes: "The coming millennium will go down in world history as a struggle between Orient and Occident, between the Church and Islam."[167]

How did Rosenzweig come to such a conclusion?

Throughout his life he tried to grasp the essence of Christianity and of Judaism, and, in the course of this search, he rediscovered his Jewish identity in 1913. Shortly afterwards, World War I broke out, during which, as a conscripted German soldier, he was stationed mostly in Macedonia, where he had contact with the local Muslim population and devoted himself to studying the Qur'an. Initially, he was influenced by the Islamic studies of Ignaz Goldziher (1850–1921) and the observations of G.W.F. Hegel (1770–1831) on Islam. In Hegel's view, Judaism and Islam belong to the same religious category, namely the "religion of the sublime." They were historically necessary stages on the way of the "Absolute Spirit". Rosenzweig later distanced himself from Hegel, about whom he had written a philosophical dissertation in the years before the First World War.

---

167 Quoted in: Palmer, Gesine and Schwartz, Yossef (Eds.). Franz Rosenzweig, "Innerlich bleibt die Welt eine" Ausgewählte Schriften zum Islam. [Inside the world remains one. Selected writings on Islam]. Philo: Berlin 2003, p. 9.

In 1914, Rosenzweig began to learn Arabic, to read the Qur'an in the original and to record his reflections. It would, of course, be wrong today to judge his ideas on the basis of the literary-critical and historical research on the Qur'an that has taken place in the meantime. Rosenzweig's aim was to grasp the essence of Islam as it was presented to him in the Qur'anic text. He was thus in the same position as the overwhelming majority of those who are exposed to the Qur'an's teachings–uninfluenced by historical-critical studies.

Rosenzweig's insights on Islam were included in his main work, *Der Stern der Erlösung* (*The Star of Redemption*), first published in 1921.[168]

Natural paganism in the form of revelation

In *The Star of Redemption*, Rosenzweig calls Islam a "remarkable case of world history plagiarism."[169] It shows, according to Rosenzweig, "what a belief in Revelation would necessarily look like when springing directly from paganism so to speak without God's will, without the plan of his providence, that is, in 'purely natural' causality. For the essential in such a purely natural emergence would be the absence of the inner inversion of the 'pre-signs' [...] His *['Muhammad's Creator']* power is shown, like the power of an oriental despot, not in the creating of the necessary [...] but in the freedom for arbitrary action."[170]

The fact that–according to Rosenzweig–Islam is, in its core "paganism," challenges the assessment that has meanwhile come to be regarded as self-evident, which puts Islam on an

---

168 Rosenzweig, Franz: The Star of Redemption. The University of Wisconsin Press: Madison, Wisconsin 2005.
169 Rosenzweig 2005, p. 128.
170 Rosenzweig 2005, p. 128.

equal footing with Judaism and Christianity, so that they are often referred to as the "three monotheistic religions" or the "Abrahamic religions." According to Rosenzweig, this imputed equality is due to the fact that Islam bears a certain resemblance to Judaism and Christianity, but he regards this as a purely outward resemblance. According to Rosenzweig, this can actually be likened to "an attempt to (re)paganize monotheism exaggerated to the point of caricature."[171]

This is not to deny that in some instances emerging Islam brought about certain improvements compared with the Arab-Bedouin ethics that preceded it. One example of such an improvement is Muhammad's ban on the then common practice of burying unwanted newborn children. On the other hand, Muhammad's fanatical zeal resulted in certain retrograde actions relative to the ethical standards of the Arab Bedouins, for example, when he had all Jewish men of the tribe of Banū Quraiza killed in 627.[172] According to Bedouin conventions, enslavement would have been enough. Compared with what had already been achieved theologically by the Jewish Christian heritage–and it is Rosenzweig's core concern to make this

---

171 Quoted from: Palmer 2003, p.14.
172 If the historicity of this massacre is acknowledged at all on the part of Islam, justification is provided in Sura 33:26–27: "And He brought down those who supported them among the People of the Scripture from their fortresses and cast terror into their hearts [so that] a party [i.e. their men] you killed, and you took captive a party [i.e. the women and children]. And He caused you to inherit their land and their homes and their properties and a land which you have not trodden. And ever is Allāh, over all things, competent." It is noteworthy that in the decades following the massacre, Islamic sources progressively decreased the numbers of those killed.

heritage fruitful once again–Islam represents a deplorable relapse into paganism.

The absence of "inner conversion"

Rosenzweig substantiates his claim of Islam as a religion that in a certain sense has developed naturally above all on the absence of the notion of "inner conversion" in Islam. "Inner conversion" occurs when the "self" of man, enclosed within itself, opens up to the hidden God. This opening up is, Rosenzweig writes, like "entering into the light of the real world."[173] The person who believes in a living, salvific God is thereby freed from his self-enclosure and is able to open himself to the voluntarily chosen unity of will with God. "Inner conversion" is consequently something completely different from "submission" to an absolutely otherworldly God.

This lack of inner conversion is shown by the way the Qur'an models certain biblical figures so that they fit the mold of exemplary–and that means fault-free–righteous figures thus becoming "worthy" precursors of Muhammad. In the Bible, on the other hand, the shortcomings and mistakes of these figures are relentlessly named, because insight into guilt and repentance are central features of biblical faith. This difference in the understanding of guilt and repentance becomes evident by looking at two biblical episodes: the critique of the installation of the Golden Calf by Aaron (Exodus 32) and the accusation against King Solomon for his involvement in idolatry (1Kn 11:5 f.). The Qur'an has, in a clear and decisive intervention, deliberately eliminated the biblical statements about the sinfulness of Aaron and Solomon.[174] Thus, in the account of

---

173 Rosenzweig 2005, p. 187.
174 Certain Muslim internet sites, such as "Jihad of the Pen," deliberately juxtapose Biblical and Qur'anic representations of

Moses' return from Mount Sinai in Sura 20:95, a "Samaritan" (Samīri) is suddenly introduced in Aaron's place as the guilty party in the golden calf episode, while Aaron gets away without the necessary repentance. As regards Solomon, it is expressly stated in Sura 2:102 that it was not he "who disbelieved." His errors are nowhere mentioned in the Qur'an–in contrast to the original biblical text.

Rosenzweig sees precisely this lack of inner conversion as a characteristic of pagan thinking and acting. It is a step backwards compared with what has already been achieved within the Judeo-Christian heritage. Where the Qur'an does refer to conversion, for example, in the description of Pharaoh drowning in the Red Sea,[175] it is in fact only referring to submission to Allāh's commands, i.e. basically to becoming a "Muslim."

The oriental despot

Rosenzweig's characterization of Allāh as an "oriental despot" is undoubtedly drastic. But by using this term, he vividly captures the image that confronted him when reading the Qur'an. There Allāh is portrayed as the supreme representative of a certain

---

Old Testament figures in order to emphasize that the "prophets" and other righteous persons in the–compared to the Bible– "unadulterated" version of the Qur'an were sinless (cf., for example: https://theartofmisinformation. wordpress.com/2011/10/05/refutation-the-quran-is-a-copy-of-the-bible/ accessed on 26/01/2022). In this they are following in the footsteps of great Islamic scholars such as Ibn Hazm (994–1064), who accused the Jews of ascribing sins to the prophets in the Torah and thus falsifying the text.

175 Cf. Sura 10:90: "[...] when drowning overtook him *[= Pharaoh]*, he said, 'I believe that there is no deity except that in whom the Children of Israel believe, and I am of the Muslims.'"

Arab-Bedouin tribal ethic, whose orders are to be obeyed absolutely. Only those who submit can hope for his "mercy." That is why, for many Muslims, Allāh is shaped by the image of mercy–since they *have* already submitted themselves to him.

The fact that an ancient Oriental ruler could demand similar sacrifices to those made in the name of Allāh to this day, can be shown by a current example: the politically and religiously motivated fight against the State of Israel consciously condones "child sacrifices," as can be read at any time in the schoolbooks of the Palestinian Authority, which, incidentally, are co-financed by the European Union. The beginning of a poem for third graders, for example, states: "I swear to sacrifice my blood to soak the land of the generous. And I will root out the occupier from my land."[176] In pagan antiquity, as we know from numerous archaeological finds in the Middle East, children were often sealed into city walls in order to gain the protection of the pagan gods during defensive struggles. Even if the context and belief systems are different now, this concept of "child sacrifice," which was demanded by an oriental tyranny, has remained the same.

The Australian professor of philosophy, Wayne Cristaudo, who examined Rosenzweig's views on Islam in detail, relates these phenomena to the person of Muhammad: "Mohammad really is a Nietzschean superman and Rosenzweig knows that the living God is not a God for supermen: the superman (believes he) has everything and is everything. What need is there for the inner humility that is part of the inner

---

176 For this and other similar examples, cf. https://www.mena-watch.com/palaestinensischer-lehrbuecher-erziehen-kinder-zu-judenhass-und-terror/ (accessed on 29/01/2019). This example also shows that it is not only the explicit terror groups such as Hamas or Hezbollah that encourage children to commit suicide attacks.

conversion?"[177] Inner humility, as Cristaudo sees it, would mean being aware of "not having and being everything."

The validity of these insights is well illustrated by the process for converting to Islam, where it is sufficient merely to publicly recite the formula of Allāh as the One and Only, and of Muhammad as his prophet. With that profession of faith, one already has everything, so to speak. There is no requirement of a process of inner conversion that would purify a person wishing to convert from the manifold pagan features of his life before being able to accept the "One" as the determining Lord of his life. Likewise, as repeatedly testified in the Qur'an, the only thing that counts at the Last Judgment in order to be able to enjoy paradise is the confession of the Islamic faith. The imaginative portrayal of the Last Judgment, for example, in Sura 56, served historically primarily to intimidate the inhabitants of Mecca, before Muhammad made his entrance as conqueror. Their conversion to Islam therefore happened under threat of death–once again, a method appropriate to an "oriental despot."

An integral, inner conversion and liberation from pagan influences, always on a voluntary basis, is not envisaged in Islam. It is not concerned with the "redemption of the world" but rather, with submission to what Rosenzweig terms a certain "oriental" system.

Parallels to an Inner-Islamic reform movement

Interestingly, some of Rosenzweig's critical thoughts about Islam coincide with certain fundamental concerns of the early

---

[177] Cristaudo, Wayne: Rosenzweig's Stance Toward Islam: The 'Troubling' Matter of the Theo-Politics in *The Star of Redemption*. In: Rosenzweig Jahrbuch Rosenzweig Yearbook 2. Karl Alber: Freiburg 2007, p. 73.

Islamic reform movement of the so-called Mu'tazilites. Their concern was "that the distinction between good and evil is independent of the will of God and all his actions are *sub ratione boni*."[178] This movement, influenced by Aristotelian philosophy, flourished from the 9th to the 11th century and then disappeared from history. It put man's freedom of will and of conscience at the center–instead of blind obedience to an "oriental despot." The fact that this Islamic perception of the need for reform had at least existed at one time shows that Rosenzweig's grasp of this unresolved issue was justified.

Redemption and revelation

Rosenzweig's observations on Islam must be read against the background of his search for new ways of understanding the biblical promise of the "redemption of the world." He is not satisfied with the view that "God's essence is thrust into a height that is foreign to the world, raised above the world,"[179] as claimed by Islam.

The Star of Redemption sees a common ground between Judaism and Christianity: The God of *creation* becomes, through *revelation*, the God of *redemption*. This is diametrically opposed to all arbitrariness. For a God thought of in terms of impenetrable transcendence, as in Islam, prevents such a redemption that is part of a process. Revelation resists "the claim of the arbitrariness of the Creator."[180] Rosenzweig once

---

178 Lehmann, Matthias: Franz Rosenzweig's Kritik des Islam im Stern der Erlösung [Franz Rosenzweig's Critique of Islam in "Star of Redemption"]. In: Jewish Studies Quarterly Vol. 1, No. 4 (1993/94). Mohr Siebeck: Princeton 1994, p. 347.
179 Rosenzweig 2005, p. 125 f.
180 Palmer 2003, p. 78.

wrote in a letter, "In Islam you will always find that God and the world always remain perfectly apart, and so either the divine disappears in the world or the world disappears in God."[181] Rosenzweig therefore concludes that the Creator God of Islam is "wealthy without any world."[182] Consequently, there is also no religiously motivated urge in Islam to participate in a comprehensive "redemption of the world." According to Islamic thinking, the world becomes a "house of peace" when it submits to Islamic rule, with further details–apparently–regulated by adherence to the Sharia.

According to Rosenzweig, it is the "arbitrariness of Allāh" in Islam that stands in sharpest contrast to the constantly renewed, instantaneous and passionate love of God for man. The appropriate response of the person so loved–according to the Judeo-Christian understanding–is a "reverence filled with humility and pride at once, a feeling of dependence and of a hidden existence, of shelter in eternal arms."[183] Islam, on the other hand, "knows a loving God just as little as it does a beloved soul,"[184] which can be seen, for example, in the meticulous compulsion to perform religious duties, which is inherent in the principle that, the more difficult an act is, the greater the devotion it demonstrates. The attachment to the

---

181 Rosenstock-Huessy, Eugen (ed.): Judaism Despite Christianity. The 1916 Wartime Correspondence between Eugen Rosenstock-Huessy and Franz Rosenzweig. With a new foreword by Paul Mendes-Flohr, a new preface by Harold Stahmer, and a new chronology by Michael Gormann-Thelen. University of Chicago Press: Chicago 2011, p. 68.
182 Rosenzweig 2005, p. 125.
183 Rosenzweig 2005, p. 182.
184 Rosenzweig 2005, p. 186. Naturally, this perception of the essence of Islam does not exclude the possibility that individual Muslims may experience things differently.

performance of duties in Judaism *does not reflect this* logic, but is motivated from elsewhere: The realization of the will of God is an expression of love for God the Eternal.

Rosenzweig presents a dynamic understanding of creation and redemption in which God seeks to reveal himself permanently. The underlying understanding of revelation is summarized by Rosenzweig expert Wayne Cristaudo as follows: "Such a conception of love [as found in Rosenzweig] requires also a revelation which is from moment to moment and is never ending, just as is creation."[185] Revelation and redemption are thus a continuous process–as opposed to a purely human defiance against such a challenge. For Rosenzweig, this is evident in pagan behavior "prior to revelation and inner conversion."[186]

Creation and redemption are, according to Rosenzweig, ongoing and historically unfinished events. Rosenzweig attributes to Judaism and Christianity the ability to engage with this continuing process of creating and redeeming the world anew. It is precisely this dynamic that he seeks to bring to light. According to Rosenzweig, the rigidity of Islam, on the other hand, is primarily due to the fact that "Muhammad took over the concepts of Revelation outwardly"[187] without grasping their dynamic nature. So for him, the notion of mankind's unfolding history with the living God is unthinkable. Rosenzweig concludes: "Islam is religion of the Book from the first moment. The Book sent down from heaven–can there be any greater distortion of the notion of God himself 'descending,' giving himself to man, of surrendering to him? He is enthroned in his highest heaven and gives to man–a Book."[188] Contrary

---

185 Cristaudo 2007, p. 70.
186 Lehmann 1994, p. 353.
187 Rosenzweig 2005, pp. 127–128.
188 Rosenzweig 2005, p. 180.

to this, the centrality of the Torah in Judaism is intimately connected with the process of its interpretation in an ongoing interpretation, to which the Talmud gives eloquent testimony.

A different realm of religious knowledge

Based on the insight that "God created precisely not religion, but rather the world,"[189] Rosenzweig attributes to Judaism and Christianity the ability to be a "revelation" *in the very midst of this world*. This revelation cannot to be thought of as a realm separate from the world. "Revelation in Rosenzweig's sense thus disenchants what enchants religion. Only when this has happened can love as an event between God, man and the world be revealed, only then can the future be thought of as open to events and to languages yet to be spoken."[190] As does his Protestant contemporary, Karl Barth (1886–1968), Rosenzweig, distinguishes between religion and revelation. In doing so he frees biblical faith from the rigidity of religion. Biblical revelation is not a separate "realm of assured knowledge about God alongside other realms of knowledge."[191] That is exactly what would be pagan. It is in this "pagan" way that the Qur'an understands the apparently inviolable "inspirations" of Muhammad: as a copy of a heavenly original. That is why its statements are positioned, without any discernible connections, i.e. "religiously," side by side with the "other areas of knowledge." From Rosenzweig's perspective, they are empty additional assertions about the

---

189 Rosenzweig, Franz: "The New Thinking" (1925). In: Franks, Paul W. and Morgan, Michael L. (Eds.): Franz Rosenzweig, Philosophical and Theological Writings. Hackett Publishing Company, Inc.: Indianapolis 2000, p. 129.
190 Palmer 2003, p. 18 f.
191 Palmer 2003, p. 21.

world–formulated in religious terms that are borrowed from Judaism and Christianity.

The effects of drawing a distinction between the realms of religious knowledge and of "worldly" knowledge extend even to current political questions. This applies both to Islamic parallel societies within democracies and to some of the statements in the Inner-Islamic *Cairo Declaration on Human Rights in Islam* of 1990. Although this document, signed by the vast majority of Islamic states, is modeled in form and content on the United Nations Universal Declaration of Human Rights and thus seems to accept this "secular" reality–it in fact places the Islamic standard, the Sharia, beside it, as if it were parallel. Article 2a, for example, states, among other things, that "it is prohibited to take away life except for a sharia prescribed reason."[192]

Conclusions from Rosenzweig's insights

Rosenzweig's view of Islam, presented here in condensed form, serves as a key to making many phenomena in Islam understandable. Rosenzweig's reference to the "oriental despot," for example, helps to explain why democratic Islamic states tend to develop dictatorial attitudes,[193] especially towards minorities, as can be seen in Turkey or Pakistan.

Of course, Rosenzweig's insights are diametrically opposed to certain basic positions that characterize the current intellectual climate in the West. Even among Rosenzweig's followers they

---

192 Source: http://hrlibrary.umn.edu/instree/cairodeclaration.html (accessed on 03/04/2022).
193 An eloquent example concerns the current President of Turkey, Recep Tayyip Erdogan who, in the 1990s, as mayor of Istanbul, was quoted as saying, "Democracy is like a tram. You ride it until you arrive at your destination, then you step off."

Franz Rosenzweig's view on Islam 113

are therefore mostly ignored or interpreted as biographically conditioned.[194] However, it was on the basis of his understanding of Judaism and Christianity that Rosenzweig dared to make statements about the "essence of Islam." Paradoxically, in the course of its history, Islam has both consciously distanced itself from Judaism and Christianity (and continues to do so today) and, at the same time, appropriated many of the elements of these two religions to construct its own identity. So, for example, the prominent Palestinian professor of philosophy, Sari Nusseibeh, said in the context of Pope Benedict's Regensburg lecture, which will be considered in the next section, "Judaeo-Christianity is nothing other than Islam"[195]–a statement which, by the way, is for Muslims fully in conformity with the Qur'an.

---

194 Cf. Schwartz, Yossef: Die entfremdete Nähe: Rosenzweigs Blick auf den Islam [The alienated proximity: Rosenzweig's view of Islam]. In: Palmer 2003, p. 146: "Rosenzweig did not develop a philosophy of religious pluralism, he did not think that there are several paths that lead to (God) the Father." It is assumed that Rosenzweig, who had previously distanced himself from Hegel's idealism, now uses his own shift in perspective to criticize Islam: "The disparagement of Islam implies a disparagement of idealism, and so Rosenzweig uses the alien religious faith to reject the familiar philosophical faith." (In: Palmer 2003, p. 144).

195 Nusseibeh, Sari: Gewalt: Rationalität und Vernünftigkeit [Violence: Rationality and Reasonableness]. In: Benedikt XVI, Glucksmann, André, Farouq, Wael, Nusseibeh, Sari, Spaemann, Robert and Weil, Joseph: Gott, rette die Vernunft! Die Regensburger Vorlesung des Papstes in der philosophischen Diskussion [God save reason! The Regensburg Address of the Pope in Philosophical Discussion]. Sankt Ulrich: Augsburg 2008, p.141. This statement of Nusseibeh's reflects the Qur'anic view of Judaism and Christianity. Consequently, questioning this view would also involve critically evaluating this source. That is also why Nusseibeh is to be challenged when he says in his response

The previously mentioned cultural philosopher, Wayne Cristaudo, summarized Rosenzweig's analysis of Islam as follows: "Franz Rosenzweig's critique of Islam is troubling. But truth is often the most troubling of things. The question is not whether what Rosenzweig says about Islam is contrary to the phantasm of Islam conjured up by well-meaning Muslim sympathizers and decent people who are Muslims. ... what matters is whether what he says is true."[196]

Interestingly, Rosenzweig judgment of Islam as a "relapse into paganism" designates a danger that often threatens Christianity when it reverts to a (semi-)pagan ways of thinking. Rosenzweig's view of Islam thus also contains the potential to be a catalyst for self-purification within Christianity itself.

A similar potential for enlightenment is contained in the statements of Pope Benedict XVI on Islam, which he succinctly expressed in his Regensburg lecture in 2006.

4.3 The Regensburg lecture of Pope Benedict XVI

Context of the speech

On 12 September 2006, Pope Benedict XVI gave a lecture ('Lectio Magistralis') at the University of Regensburg, Germany, where he had been professor of theology from 1969 to 1977. In that landmark lecture under the title "Faith, Reason and the

---

to the Regensburg address of Pope Benedict XVI that what this should have dealt with are the misguided practices in all religions, "and not with what has been handed down to us in the Holy Books." (Nusseibeh, ibid., p. 142).

196 Cristaudo 2007, p. 50.

The Regensburg lecture of Pope Benedict XVI   115

University–Memories and Reflections"[197] he also addressed the question of the "God of rationality" in Islam and in biblical faith. The reaction to the lecture by the Muslim world was largely negative and, in some cases, violent. The anger was triggered by a passage at the beginning of the speech, where the Pope quoted a statement of the Byzantine Emperor Manuel II Paleologus of 1391, in one of his conversations with a Persian Muslim interlocutor on the central question of the relationship between religion and violence. After remarking that the Byzantine Emperor had addressed his interlocutor "with a brusqueness that we find unacceptable," the Pope quoted the following statement of the emperor: "Show me just what Muhammad brought that was new, and there you will find things only evil and inhuman, such as his command to spread by the sword the faith he preached."[198]

The Pope's reflections on the relationship between rationality and the nature of God are central to the speech. They presuppose that the question of truth[199] may be legitimately raised and that

---

197 The text of the lecture is available at: https://www.vatican.va/cont ent/benedict-xvi/en/speeches/2006/september/documents/hf_ben-xvi_spe_20060912_university-regensburg.html (accessed on 01/ 02/2022). All quotations from this lecture in the present text are taken from this source.

198 In an interview in 2010, Benedict XVI commented on this controversy and the violent consequences of his lecture about which, he said, "I can only feel sadness:" "The political reading ignored the fine web of the argument, ripping the passage out of its context and turning it into a political statement, which it wasn't. The text dealt with an exchange in an ancient dialogue, which, incidentally, I think is still of great interest." (In: Benedict XVI: Light of the World. A Conversation with Peter Seewald. Catholic Truth Society: London 2010, p. 97).

199 The rejection of the question of truth is based above all on the philosophical notion of *Deconstruction* which considers

it has nothing to do with intolerance or violent enforcement. It may be worth noting in this regard that the 19th century German philosopher G.W.F. Hegel warned that "philosophy must beware of the wish to be edifying,"[200] saying that it should, rather, be guided by the desire of reason, in order to strive for knowledge of truth.

The vastness of reason

Pope Benedict XVI bases the rejection of violence on the very essence of God himself. The starting point of his argumentation is the insight of Manuel II Paleologus (1350–1425) that "God is not pleased by blood–and not acting reasonably (σὺν λόγω) [= syn logo] is contrary to God's nature. Faith is born of the soul, not the body. Whoever would lead someone to faith needs the ability to speak well and to reason properly, without violence and threats... To convince a reasonable soul, one does not need a strong arm, or weapons of any kind, or any other means of threatening a person with death." This quotation from Manuel II

---

       this question neither desirable nor possible, and in any case fundamentally relative. Nevertheless, some positive inspiration may be drawn from Friedrich Nietzsche (1844–1900), who wrote (in: Die Fröhliche Wissenschaft [The Gay Science]) that "even we knowing ones of today, the godless and the anti-metaphysical, still take our fire from the conflagration kindled by a belief a millennium old, the Christian belief, which was also the belief of Plato, that God is truth, that the truth is divine." (Quoted in: Robert Spaemann, Gedanken zur Regensburger Vorlesung [in: God, save reason, Sankt Ulrich Verlag: Augsburg, 2008], p. 161).

200 In: Hegel, G.W.F.: Phenomenology of Spirit. Oxford University Press: Oxford 1977, Preface, 9.

Paleologus is the starting point for the Pope's further reflections on the relationship of Faith and Reason.

The reasonableness of God has its biblical foundation in the prologue of John, in which everything starts from the Logos. Pope Benedict specifies what is meant by this "Logos"–traditionally translated as "the Word." "*Logos* means both reason and word– a reason which is creative and capable of self-communication, precisely as reason."

In this prologue of John, enlightened Greek thought and the biblical message find a synthesis that had its beginning in the Old Testament. The developmental arc of the "encounter of faith and reason ..., an encounter between genuine enlightenment and religion" spans, so Pope Benedict further explains, the whole of the Old Testament: from the revelation of God at the Burning Bush–which was connected with a historical mission and therefore overcomes mythological religiosity–to the unmasking of pagan gods in the Babylonian exile, up to the wisdom literature of the Hellenistic age.

In a short exposition Pope Benedict then shows that the intellectual impasse represented by God's *irrationality* existed not only in the Islamic tradition[201] but also in the history of Christian theology. But the church tradition as a whole "has always insisted that between God and us, between his eternal Creator Spirit and our created reason there exists a real analogy". Even if this analogy remains subject to the reservation that, according to Pope Benedict, "unlikeness remains infinitely greater than likeness" and even if love transcends mere thought (cf. Eph 3:19), "nonetheless it continues to be love of the God who

---

201 As proof, Benedict refers to the great Islamic scholar Ibn Hazm (994–1064), who claimed that Allāh is not bound by anything. In Pope Benedict's words, "Were it God's will, we would even have to practice idolatry."

is *Logos*. Consequently, Christian worship is [...] 'λογικη λατρεία' [= logike latreia, i.e. 'reasonable worship'], worship in harmony with the eternal Word and with our reason (cf. Rom 12:1)."

In this way, the Pope makes clear that a rational image of God is reflected in a correspondingly rational form of divine service. This, we can add in the sense of his other remarks on this subject,[202] results in a rational world order. The Pope concludes the lecture with an urgent appeal for the "courage to engage in the whole breadth of reason" as a basis for a deepened "dialogue of cultures."

Deepening our knowledge of God

The goal of such a dialogue is to deepen our knowledge of God. Even if there were irrational tendencies in the history of Christian theology, there is a way out. Thus, the Pope established a bridge with the Islamic world aiming towards the "logic of God," and, more specifically, towards a *common* God. Similar to Rosenzweig, Pope Benedict tries to overcome the division between the realm of the "knowledge of God" and the realm of scientific thinking in general. It is also possible for Islam to participate in the encounter between Judaism and Greek philosophy, like Christianity before it. It could thereby broaden its perspective.

That would also be a way of overcoming the problematic concept of the so-called "double truth" developed by the Islamic philosopher, Averroës (1126–1198). This refers to the division into "on the one hand, the truth expressed by philosophers in the language of logic and reason, and, on the other hand, the

---

202 Cf. on this subject: Pope Benedict XVI: The Spirit of the Liturgy. Ignatius Press: San Francisco 2015.

truth expressed by the general public in the language of allegory and religion."[203]

Initiatives to overcome the "double truth" concept already exist in Islamic tradition itself. In the Middle Ages, mediated by Nestorian circles and despite initial resistance from orthodox Islamic scholars, the works of classical Greek philosophers were translated into Arabic. They were thus integrated into the Muslim world and its canon of knowledge, and subsequently found their way into medieval European philosophy and theology. So there had already been a time in history, albeit a short one, when Islamic theology and Greek philosophy *coexisted*. If this connection were to be "rehabilitated" within Islam, the Pope's reference to the "reasonableness" of God could be the decisive argument in repudiating any propensity to violence in the name of religion. Striving to deepen our knowledge of God and his inherent reasonableness thus contains a great potential for hope.

Obstacles to understanding

Many Muslim reactions to the Pope's lecture showed, however, that the concept of the reasonableness of God as expressed by the Logos is hardly comprehensible from the Islamic perspective. Since, according to the Qur'an, Allāh also created reason, the latter cannot–following this logic–stand in opposition to Allāh. That is, because in traditional Islamic understanding, the Muslim attains reason "by inspiration,"[204] which is fed by memory, language and virtues. Moreover, the Arabic term *reason* (`aql) is primarily connected with the meaning "to tie up, to restrict, to

---

203 Nusseibeh 2008, p. 123. Cf. footnote 194.
204 Farouq, Wael: Zu den Wurzeln der arabischen Vernunft [On the roots of Arabic reason]. In: God, Save Reason, p. 77. (cf. footnote 194).

hold in check"–this word also designates the reins of the camel– and thus refers primarily to holding the tongue in check.[205]

Individual voices from the Islamic world, however, have acknowledged that the Pope's lecture touched on a highly relevant issue, namely, the rift in the Arab world between modernity and tradition. In this context, it is encouraging that efforts were subsequently made to find a common Islamic response to the Regensburg lecture. Such a reaction has not been elicited by any speech of a Pope before or since.

One of the prominent responses to the Regensburg lecture stands out: an open letter of 138 Muslim scholars to Christian leaders entitled "A Common Word Between Us and You,"[206] published in autumn 2007. In this document, these scholars emphasized above all the uniqueness of God and the resulting "love of neighbor" as a common Muslim-biblical heritage.[207] The document closes with an appeal for mutual respect, without, however, going into the question raised by Pope Benedict about the reasonableness of God. The litmus test here would have been the unequivocal rejection of any kind of coercion, as expressed by Pope Benedict in his quote from Emperor Manuel II Paleologus: "Faith is born of the soul, not the body. Whoever

---

205 Cf. the detailed explanations in Farouq, ibid. 77 f.
206 The English translation is available online at: https://www.acom monword.com/wp-content/uploads/2018/05/ACW-English-Tran slation.pdf (accessed on 21/02/2022). This explanation took place one year after the open letter of 38 Muslim scholars to Pope Benedict, in which they above all tried to explain God's transcendence, the use of reason and the use of violence from an Islamic perspective.
207 Here they are following a line of argument already expressed by the medieval Islamic scholar, Ibn Hazm, mentioned in the Regensburg speech: "For Ibn Hazm, it is not so much reason [...] as love that rules the world!" (Nusseibeh 2008, p. 125).

would lead someone to faith needs the ability to speak well and to reason properly, without violence and threats".[208]

From the Islamic side, reference is often made in this regard–especially in the Western context–to the introductory sentence of Sura 2:256: "There shall be no compulsion in [acceptance of] the religion." However, to regard this as an Islamic endorsement of freedom of religion can only come about if one considers this verse in isolation and on the basis of the individualistic understanding of religion common in the West. Verse 256 taken in its entirety, and verse 257 which follows it, are, in fact, a stark warning to the Gentiles of the consequences of the failure to convert to Islam.[209] The end of verse 257 reads: "As for the unbelievers, their patrons are the idols: They lead them from the light to the folds of darkness. These are the people of the Fire, in which they abide forever."[210]

---

208 In the 2010 interview (cf. footnote 198), Pope Benedict XVI looks back on the fact that the realization within Islam of the need to clarify the questions concerning its relation to violence and its relation to reason, had led to an internal reflection among Muslim scholars. However, that important question still needs to be resolved: "At issue are questions such as: What is tolerance? How are truth and tolerance related? In this context, the question of whether tolerance includes the right to change religions also emerges. It is hard for the Islamic partners to accept this. Their argument is that once someone has come to the truth, he can no longer turn back. At any rate, we have entered into an extensive and vigorous relation of dialogue that is bringing us closer and teaching us to understand one another better. Which also just may help us to find more positive ways of facing this difficult hour of history together." (Benedict XVI 2010, p. 99).

209 Cf. the corresponding references by T. Nagel (in: What is Islam? p. 44; cf. footnote 180).

210 Tarif Khalidi translation; cf. footnote 99.

4.4 Summary and outlook

The statements of Franz Rosenzweig and Joseph Ratzinger on Islam stem from two different epochs and contexts–and yet they display astonishing convergences.

The first of these is their fundamental view of Islam as a "relapse": into paganism according to Rosenzweig, whereas according to Pope Benedict, it is a relapse into an irrationality and the associated compulsion that bears no resemblance to the heights of the biblical image of God. This regression was due in part to the fact that state and religion were equated with each other, a situation already identified by the then Cardinal Ratzinger in an interview in 2003: "For up to Christ the identification of religion and state, of deity and state, was almost necessary to give stability to the state. Then Islam returns to this identification of the political world and the religious world, based on the assumption that it is only by means of political power that humanity can be moralized."[211]

What Rosenzweig describes as a relapse into paganism and thus a shift away from the dynamics of the biblical message, becomes for Pope Benedict an invitation to everyone–including Muslims–to open themselves freely to reason, which is accessible to all, and to its vastness. On the other hand, Pope Benedict also appeals to "secular reason" not to shut itself off from theological traditions. Retaining such openness would even, "where Islam has a [...] monocultural dominance," as Pope Benedict explained in an interview some years after the Regensburg lecture, deprive Islam of the perception that it alone is "the defender [...] of religion against atheism and secularism."[212]

---

[211] From the conversation with Antonio Socci (Il Giornale 2003). In: Ratzinger, Joseph: Gesammelte Schriften [Collected Works] 13/3. Herder: Freiburg 2017, p. 1416 f.
[212] Benedict XVI 2010, p. 101.

In the Regensburg lecture, Joseph Ratzinger/Pope Benedict XVI showed the extent to which the biblical tradition converges with and is conducive to rational ways of thinking and acting. In *The Star of Redemption*, Rosenzweig unfolds the dynamics of the biblical message in a philosophical discourse guided by reason.

What perspectives result from this?

Rosenberg and Ratzinger have demonstrated that both the biblical message and reason must first be rediscovered in a new and convincing way in order for their dynamics to become effective. Genuine dialogue between cultures, as called for by Pope Benedict and as promoted by Pope Francis in his own particular way, could be advanced by following the path of reason–*beyond submission* and thus beyond any restrictions on freedom of thought.

Franz Rosenzweig seems justified in his assessment, made a hundred years ago, that the "struggle between East and West, Church and Islam" would shape the current millennium. Looking afresh at Rosenzweig's philosophical-theological response to Islam could be of decisive help in considering the issues raised.

Further developing the insights of Pope Benedict XVI that acting in accordance with the Logos is in keeping with the very nature of God is a similarly worthy millennium project–a task of the utmost importance both for Christianity itself and for any realistic dialogue with Islam.

This book seeks to make a contribution to these endeavors.

Bibliography

Abramowski, Luise et al. (Ed.): A Nestorian Collection of Christological Texts. Volumes I–II, Cambridge University Press: Cambridge 1972

Akhtar, Shabbir: Islam as Political Religion. Routledge: London 2011

Andrae, Tor: Der Ursprung des Islams und das Christentum. Almquist & Wiksells: Uppsala, 1926 [Hildesheim: ²1977]

Babylonian Talmud: The William Davidson Talmud: https://www.sefaria.org/Sanhedrin.37b?lang=bi (accessed on 17/11/2019)

Benedikt XVI.: Faith, Reason and the University. Memories and Reflections. In: https://www.vatican.va/content/benedict-xvi/en/speeches/2006/september/documents/hf_ben-xvi_spe_20060912_university-regensburg.html (accessed on 01/02/2022)

Benedict XVI: Light of the World. A Conversation with Peter Seewald. Catholic Truth Society: London 2010

Busse, Heribert: Islam, Judaism and Christianity: Theological and Historical Affiliations. Markus Wiener Publishers: Princeton, N.J. 1998

Cairo Declaration on Human Rights in Islam. 1988. In: http://hrlibrary.umn.edu/instree/cairodeclaration.html (accessed on 03/04/2022)

Clooney, Francis X.: Comparative Theology: Deep Learning Across Religious Borders. Wiley-Blackwell: Chichester 2010

Colpe Carsten: Das Siegel der Propheten. Historische Beziehungen zwischen antikem Judentum, Judenchristentum, Heidentum und frühem Islam. Arbeiten zur neutestamentlichen Theologie und Zeitgeschichte. ANTZ Band 3: Berlin 2006

Cristaudo, Wayne: Rosenzweig's Stance Toward Islam: The 'Troubling' Matter of the Theo-Politics in *The Star of Redemption*. In: Rosenzweig Jahrbuch Rosenzweig Yearbook 2. Karl Alber: Freiburg 2007

Denzinger, Heinrich (Ed.): Enchiridion Symbolorum, Definitionum et Declarationum in rebus fidei et morum. Herder: Freiburg ³³1965

Faith and Inculturation. International Theological Commission 1988. In: https://www.vatican.va/roman_curia/congregations/cfaith/cti_documents/rc_cti_1988_fede-inculturazione_en.html (accessed on 15/03/2020)

Glucksmann, André et al. (Ed.): Benedict XVI. Gott, rette die Vernunft. Die Regensburger Vorlesung des Papstes in der philosophischen Diskussion. Sankt Ulrich: Augsburg 2008

Gnilka, Joachim: Bibel und Koran. Herder: Freiburg 2004

Hartwig, Dirk et al.: Im vollen Licht der Geschichte. Ergon: Würzburg 2008

Infancy Gospel of James: http://www.earlychristianwritings.com/text/infancyjames-roberts.html (accessed on 21/02/2022)

Infancy Gospel of Thomas: http://www.earlychristianwritings.com/text/infancythomas.html (accessed on 21/01/2022)

Khadduri, Majid: War and Peace in the Law of Islam. The Lawbook Exchange: Clark/New Jersey 2006

Lehmann, Matthias: Franz Rosenzweigs Kritik des Islam im „Stern der Erlösung". In: Jewish Studies Quarterly Vol. 1, No. 4 (1993/94). Mohr Siebeck: Princeton 1994

Lumen Gentium. Dogmatic Constitution on the Church, Vatican Council II, 21 November 1964, No. 9. https://www.vatican.va/archive/hist_councils/ii_vatican_council/documents/vat-ii_const_19641121_lumen-gentium_en.html (accessed on 21/04/2020)

Lustiger, Jean-Marie: Choosing God, Chosen by God. Ignatius Press: San Francisco 1991

Lustiger, Jean-Marie: The Promise. Wm. B. Eerdmans Publishing Co.: Grand Rapids, Michigan/Cambridge, U.K. 2007

Maier, Bernhard: Koran-Lexikon. Kröner: Stuttgart 2001

Mani/Manichäismus. In: Lexikon für Theologie und Kirche. Band 6. Herder: Freiburg 2009, S. 1266

Nagel, Tilman: Was ist der Islam? Grundzüge einer Weltreligion. Duncker&Humblot: Berlin 2018

Nestorius/ Nestorianismus. In: Lexikon für Theologie und Kirche. Band 7. Herder: Freiburg 2009, p. 747

Neuwirth, Angelika: Koranforschung–eine politische Philologie? De Gruyter: Berlin 2014

Neuwirth, Angelika: The Qur'an and Late Antiquity: A Shared Heritage. Oxford University Press: New York 2019

Nostra aetate. Declaration on the Relation of the Church to Non-Christian Religions, No 4: http://www.vatican.va/archive/hist_councils/ii_vatican_council/documents/vat-ii_decl_19651028_nostra-aetate_en.html (accessed on 04/03/2022)

Palmer, Gesine and Schwartz, Yossef (Eds.). Franz Rosenzweig, "Innerlich bleibt die Welt eine" Ausgewählte Schriften zum Islam. Philo: Berlin 2003

Räisänen, Heikki: Das koranische Jesusbild. Ein Beitrag zur Theologie des Korans. Finnische Gesellschaft für Missiologie und Ökumenik: Helsinki 1971

Ratzinger, Joseph: Gesammelte Schriften JRGS 13/3. Herder: Freiburg 2017

Reynolds, Gabriel Said (Ed.): The Qur'an in Its Historical Context. Routledge: London 2008

Reynolds, Gabriel Said: The Qur'an and Its Biblical Subtext. Routledge: London 2010

Roncaglia, M. P.: Élements Ébionites et Elkésaites dans le Coran. In: POC [Proche-Orient Chretien] 21: Jerusalem 1971

Rosenstock-Huessy, Eugen (Ed.): Judaism Despite Christianity. The 1916 Wartime Correspondence between Eugen Rosenstock-Huessy and Franz Rosenzweig. University of Chicago Press: Chicago 2011

Rosenzweig, Franz: "The New Thinking" (1925). In: Franks, Paul W. and Morgan, Michael L. (Eds.): Franz Rosenzweig, Philosophical and Theological Writings. Hackett Publishing Company, Inc.: Indianapolis 2000

Rosenzweig, Franz: The Star of Redemption. The University of Wisconsin Press: Madison, Wisconsin 2005

Simon, Róbert: Mani and Muhammad. JSAI (Jerusalem Studies in Arabic and Islam) 21: Jerusalem 1997

Speyer, Heinrich: Die biblischen Erzählungen im Qoran. Olms: Hildesheim 2013

Stötzel, Arnold: Verstehen der jüdisch-christlichen Offenbarung angesichts des Islam. In: Heute in Kirche und Welt 1/2002 und 2/2002. Bad Tölz 2002

The Qur'an–A New Translation by Tarif Khalidi. Penguin Classics: London 2009

The Qur'ān–English Meanings. English Revised and Edited by Ṣaḥeeḥ International. In: https://asimiqbal2nd.files.wordpress.com/2009/06/quran-sahih-international.pdf (accessed on 28/03/2022)

Von Stosch, Klaus, Khorchide, Mouhanad (Eds.): Streit um Jesus: Muslimische und christliche Annäherungen. Schöningh: Paderborn 2016

Von Stosch, Klaus: Zur Lage Komparativer Theologie. In: Theologische Revue 2019 Nr. 5. Hrsg. Katholisch-Theologische Fakultät der Universität Münster: Münster 2019

Weimer, Ludwig: Die Lust an Gott und seiner Sache. Herder: Freiburg 1981

www.ingramcontent.com/pod-product-compliance
Lightning Source LLC
Chambersburg PA
CBHW020334170426
43200CB00006B/384